Praise for *To My Children's Children*

"Magona's memoir is a delightful, poignant, feisty and uplifting story that chronicles, in a refreshing and authentic voice, what it means to attain womanhood in a society where patriarchy and apartheid often conspired to degrade and enslave women economically, domestically, politically, traditionally and sexually."
— ***Washington Post Book World***

"Sindiwe Magona writes with vibrance and intimacy. [She] offers the reader deep insight into life under apartheid."
— *Everywoman* (U.K.)

"Reading Sindiwe Magona's celebratory autobiography is like holding a handful of bright African beads; each tale and her telling of it is part of the treasure; you are affected and altered... It is a bold, spirited, funny book... one of the best..."
— *Argus*

"Her tale is about a special past; about the joys, pains, love and enmity which befalls blacks in varying degrees, and at the various levels of human conduct... I read and relished Magona's vividly written account about her sheltered and protected childhood; about the pain and trauma of dislocation, schooling, death and womanhood... the crystal-clear voice of a dignified, proud yet humble, and graceful woman. A book to read."
— *The Weekly Mail* (S.A.)

"It is extremely difficult for a black writer to maintain a sense of humor and optimism when writing about life in South Africa... Sindiwe Magona's sensitive and lively account of her childhood and early adulthood, however, is refreshingly free from the characteristic self-pitying sentimentality which sometimes weakens the powerful social criticism this kind of writing intends to make... such powerful self-revelation finally confirms that this emergent writer has set new standards for protest writing."
— *South*

"Not only is Magona's story worth telling, but her use of language is so masterly that it becomes a delight in itself... [A] highly readable book. Incidents are always recounted with humour and wit and her descriptions of people she meets is nothing short of inspired."
— *Literary Review*

"More than simply an account of her own life, Sindiwe Magona's *To My Children's Children* is a reflection of the struggle faced by all black South African women not only against Apartheid but also against their own culture and people... It's gripping and comprehensive, dragging the reader from sympathy to sorrow, laughter to anger... Sindiwe Magona could become the next cult name amongst black women writers — she certainly has some stories to tell."
— **Laura Manison**
University of Cardiff

"Autobiography at its finest, where the self-portrait also becomes a canvas of a suppressed people, writing in dignity... struggling for justice and a new nationhood."
— *Morning Star*

"This is no ordinary autobiography. It is a pulsating, intimate adventure into the life of a South African woman who endured life under apartheid."

— *Response*

"Her vivid descriptions of Xhosa customs unfold not as an anthropologist's field study but as a memory etched from experience."

— *Publishers Weekly*

"Her book may be written to her children's children, but its messages go beyond bloodlines. It has something to say to the global family about the ravages of racism, the strength of family and the perseverance of the African spirit."

— *The Boston Globe*

Praise for *Living, Loving and Lying Awake at Night*

"Sindiwe Magona's *Living, Loving and Lying Awake at Night* rips away apartheid's shroud which hovers over lives, loves and losses of South African women with a ferocity that is both startling and enlightening... [It] is a riveting look at the triumph of will and spirit in the face of apartheid's dehumanization. Magona has given us endearing characters and probing stories that are as authoritative as they are unforgettable.

— *Quarterly Black Review of Books*

"Magona is a storyteller centered in her power, convinced of the universal relevance of what she sees. The effect is felt like the strong South African sun, each story's momentum like the pounding of a drum."

— *Booklist*

"Her book is of excruciating beauty and yet covered by a mantle of hope and love... From the very first lines of this book you know you are in the hands of a powerful wordmaker..."

— *Morning Star* (U.K.)

"Living, Loving and Lying Awake at Night confirms her ability to speak on behalf of African women with an acuity that is frequently very funny, often achingly sad... Magona's rendition of the tragicomedy of the lives of disadvantaged South African women is so sharply done one can almost believe it's all fiction."

— *Cosmopolitan* (U.K.)

"The outstanding feature of *Living, Loving and Lying Awake at Night* is the style: a soliloquy which rarely becomes a dialogue."

— *World Literature Today*

"A superb collection of short stories bringing a full range of South African women's experiences brilliantly to light... this collection is at once tragic, triumphant, humorous and sharp, but above all, forcefully empowering."

— *Feminist Bookstore News*

Forced to Grow

SINDIWE MAGONA

INTERLINK BOOKS

An imprint of Interlink Publishing Group, Inc.

NEW YORK

First American edition published 1998 by

INTERLINK BOOKS
An imprint of Interlink Publishing Group, Inc.
99 Seventh Avenue
Brooklyn, New York 11215

Originally published in South Africa by
David Philip Publishers (Pty) Ltd.

Library of Congress Cataloging-in-Publication Data

Magona, Sindiwe.
    Forced to grow / Sindiwe Magona.
        p.   cm.
    ISBN 1-56656-265-1
    1. Magona, Sindiwe—Biography. 2. Women authors, South African—
20th century—Biography. 3. Women teachers—South African—
Biography. 4. Single-parent family—South Africa. I. Title.
    PR9369.3.M335Z466 1998
    823—dc21   97-17848
    [B]   CIP

Printed and bound in Canada

10 9 8 7 6 5 4 3 2 1

KUMAMA

Phambi kwenyawo zakho, Ntumbeza,
ndendlala ezimbeje-mbeje
zon'iintyathyambo; ezivumba limyoli;
ezikuthamba buboya bemvu – ukuze
ungaze wahlatywa nkqu naliliva:
Kuba wandinika ubomi.
Wandondla. Wandoluleka.

TO MOTHER

Before your feet, Ntumbeza,
I spread thousands of flowers of brightest
hues, of most delightful scent,
soft as wool of lamb – that you may
never tread on even a thorn.
For you gave me life.
You fed, body and soul.

One

I was a has-been at the age of twenty-three. Sans husband, I was the mother of two little girls and expecting my third child – as it turned out, a son. He was born in October 1966, four months after his father had left us.

In my memory, the year 1967 wears a yellow. Not too bright a yellow. No. A soft and shy yellow, tentative as the hope I could not but nurse. Too bright a yellow, too strong a hope, I could not afford. It would have frightened me no end to harbour a hope that bold: too much to lose.

Too soon I had learnt to dream small dreams, trust less, and fear in abundance.

The English language is kinder than mine. A has-been, even at the tender age at which I found myself one, still does imply some prior accomplishment; 'being' that which one no longer is: a previous, if lost, glory. Xhosa, my mother tongue, brutal in clarity regarding matters of this nature, provided me with no such comforting ambiguity.

Umabuy'ekwendeni – a returnee from wifehood – was my new designation; and I was doomed thereafter to *idikazi* which, according to the Reverend Robert Godfrey's *A Kaffir-English Dictionary* (printed in 1918), refers to 'an unmarried female'. And, the dictionary further enlightens us, this is 'a term of reproach to all women who are husbandless'. And that, I certainly was.

Moreover, if I had any notion that I might escape the condemnation of society, this dictionary told me such reprieve was not for the likes of me. Only widows are exempt from the withering term, it says. But that is not to say any old widow is automatically above rebuke. No. She has to be a good widow. Only those 'widows who have not left the places of their late husbands' does society deem good. What hope had I? My husband was not late nor had I remained in 'his place'. This would have been impossible even had I wanted to do so: at the time that he left me, my husband could not have established a residence in the Cape Town area. He did not qualify. Because he did not meet government conditions, he was not allowed to rent a council house in Langa or Nyanga or Guguletu. And I, a woman, could never hope for that basic right. This because, in the eyes of the law, I was a minor. Moreover, had he left me and the children in 'his place', how would I have paid the rent? Thus, both from a purely practical point of view and according to society's moral standards, I was in a no-win situation. *Idikazi.*

It seemed a little unfair, if not downright unjust, that it was I, left to fend for myself and three young children, who had somehow lost society's esteem. I knew then no equivalent term for a man. More than twenty years later, not only have I not discovered it in Xhosa, it has eluded me in the three other languages I speak.

Such was my status as 1967 began. The two-month-old baby and his two little sisters had only me. And I, husbandless, with neither job nor access to any money, had only blind, unreasonable, fragile hope.

A social polecat, a woman of dubious repute, I was jobless in a country with a myriad of laws, none of which was of any benefit to me or mine. As an African I was not covered by any social security laws. Indeed, the laws that did cover me did so only to my detriment.

I lived in the Western Cape, in Guguletu, one of the three African townships closest to the city of Cape Town. If Africans did not enjoy equal access to opportunity throughout the country, for some reason Africans in this part of the country had been dished out additional hardship. The government, in its infinite wisdom, had declared the Western Cape a 'Coloured Preferential Area'. And that boiled down to the simple fact that employers were not legally allowed to offer jobs to Africans until after they had ascertained that no coloured person (in South African terms, a person of mixed race) was available to fill that position. Of course, job discrimination is known elsewhere in the world, but South Africa must surely hold the dubious honour of having legally created unemployment.

When things become really bad, people usually get into debt. I was saved from that ruinous path since a minor could not enter into contracts. But even without this I would have been safe. To borrow from banks one needed to put up surety, usually immovable property, a house – a house one owned. As Africans were not allowed to own immovable property in the urban areas, I was thus doubly insured against ever getting into trouble that way.

The second half of 1966 had been an abysmal hole of hopelessness. My husband's desertion had plunged me from poverty into destitution. So at the beginning of 1967 I took, like a lover to my bosom, emaciated, wary, shadowy hope. I reckoned, without any foundation, that 1967 had to be better. 1966 had been a lean, mean, wolfishly gnawing year; my confidence its fare.

One consolation was mine though. The children were too young to know what they were going through, I told myself. Long-term effects were far from my mind. Pressing were the needs of today.

I eked out an existence so we would not starve to death. Fortunately for me, I had grown up in a home with decisively effective parents. I had a father who took his role of provider seriously and Mother had never known an idle moment in her life. Unless ill in bed, she was always, always trying to augment the family income. I could have done much worse than have a woman like that as a role model, and in my hour of dire need I unconsciously fell back on some of those ways of making money I had witnessed as I was growing up.

Until I was about sixteen, every Saturday and Sunday during rugby season I sold ginger beer, *ebaleni*, at the rugby field, the straggly patch of common our teams used. This was not a task I relished. I was not the only ginger-beer seller there, and competition was stiff, the players grouchy, stingy with compliments but very free with complaints and condemnation. One tiny ant in a bottle was enough to make a player come striding over and yell: 'I want my money back. Look!' And every player and every spectator would stop whatever they had been doing and all these grown-up eyes would turn to look at me while the hole I was praying for refused to open up and swallow me live. Meanwhile, another customer would complain there wasn't enough sugar in the ginger beer whilst yet another grumbled because the ginger beer was too sweet. I hated the rugby season with all my heart. I hated ginger beer. And, as long as I live, unless compelled, I will not sell anything to anyone. Now, however, need forced me to forget my antipathy. I needed money, so I made and sold ginger beer.

It was not long before I understood why we had never got to be millionaires when I was a child selling ginger beer for my mother. The trickle that came from twenty-four bottles of ginger beer (all that came from a four-gallon tin's brew) sold with luck, over three to four days was ant spittle. Moreover, most times I gave bottles and bottles away or drank some as the ginger beer threatened to sour. And even lovers of the stuff drank very little ginger beer in the cool of that winter.

Mother had taught her lessons well. To this day her injunctions set her apart in the society of Guguletu. And these injunctions were frequent, vigorous and biting. I grew up well aware that *iimpundu ziyavimba!* – 'buttocks are stingy'; that is, one gained nothing by using that part of one's body too much.

I believed in stirring myself and as soon as I saw that the ginger-beer business was taking me nowhere fast, I backed off and instead baked and sold *vetkoek*, scrubbed, cooked and sold sheep heads and found, once more, that I was still not making ends meet. Indeed, the ends were so far apart that when I stood near one, the other was clear out of sight. Then I had not a brainwave but a bout of bravado, a dance with daring, undiluted stupidity.

It all started with a little recklessness. Granted, the act was born of desperation but it was, nonetheless, one of profound indiscretion for me. But let's start with the venial sin, the one that led to what I would never have thought of doing ... under any circumstances.

Finding my attempts at self-employment unsatisfactory, I turned to selling liquor. This I soon abandoned, though not through any scruples on my part. Before long I saw that this was a high-risk business, on two counts. Not only was it illegal to sell liquor but customers took what they wanted during the week on credit. Fridays, when they were paid, they came to pay. At least, that was the general understanding. I found out, however, that the numbness which these camels sought and which eluded them throughout the week was somehow theirs on Fridays.

On Fridays, shebeen queens are lucky if fifty per cent of their customers show up. Pockets bulging with their wages, the guzzlers, blinded by this immense wealth, forget the miserable women who kept them oiled during the week. On Fridays their dulled eyes lead them astray, to the wives who, during the week, waited with cold enticements that failed to lure them home.

Paid, these gentlemen buy from white-owned 'Cash 'n Carry' bottle-stores where no one will know their names by Sunday when, once again, they appear at the door of the shebeen, parched and begging. I may have become a little prejudiced against men, it is hard to say. But women appeared to pay better, more promptly and less grudgingly.

The fact that women, when they bought on credit, were by and large buying food to be shared by the whole family may account for their ability to pay on pay-day. The sponging husband, on the other hand, could have found it a little problematic to explain the disappearance of nearly half his pay. Even the rare husband who still honoured his wife with a sealed pay envelope on Fridays either lacked the courage to demand that much from his pay or, I discovered belatedly (and to my ruin), had enjoyed too much of Victoria's Tears to be able to wipe every slate clean. A sobering thought for me. But I didn't realise the position until it was very nearly too late.

One day I was talking to a neighbour about my unenviable plight, trying to convince her that hers was a much healthier state compared with mine. The poor woman, in her late thirties, had been recently abandoned by her husband after more than twenty years of marriage. Of course, he left her with their four teenage children, all boys, all in high school. But, wallowing in my own misery, I could see no calamity as harsh as mine or need as deep. That her husband sometimes gave her money was enough to make me oblivious to her suffering.

'Why don't you do as I do? Sell tobacco?' asked the woman while my eyes popped out and grew stalks the size of young carrots.

'Sell *dagga* [marijuana]? Me?' To say I was utterly flabbergasted would be putting it mildly. *Dagga*, 'tobacco' as the euphemism goes in the African townships, is an illegal substance.

Yes, I had been illegally selling liquor. However, for me there was, in an unformed way, a very big difference between selling a nip of brandy and a *zoll* of marijuana. Whether this perception had anything to do with the scale of punishment attached to the two I can't say, but although I knowingly risked arrest for selling liquor, I was far from ready to risk being arrested for selling *dagga*. Could it be that I saw the one as more immoral than the other? More sinful? More destructive?

I doubt that there is a sadder sight in the whole wide world than that of a starving child. Need is a terrible thing and when it engulfs the very young, the most vulnerable, it eats into one's very heart, especially if that heart is that of a mother. The plight of my children, the sales talk of this woman, time and hopelessness finally made me 'see reason', as my mentor said.

One evening, this lady came to see me 'with an offer you cannot refuse'. For fifty rand, she would procure a whole bag of the stuff for me. A small bag, yes, but a bag nonetheless. Enough for me to realise ten times what I was laying out. 'It's just that that dog, Lizo's father, did not give me anything this week. Otherwise I would be taking all this stuff for myself.' She did not want to disappoint her supplier, she said. If he brought her order, it was her part of the bargain to pay the agreed amount. All of it. 'Otherwise what is the poor man to do with the stuff? He can't return it, you know.' My benefactor could not have been more helpful. Had I a bankbook, I'd have started filling out the deposit slip. For five hundred rand. Not only was I getting this bag at tremendous discount, she would help me sell the stuff. 'As soon as I've sold one bag, I'll come and take from you whenever a customer comes.'

Where, then, was any risk for me? Her explanation made perfectly good sense too. She was not just being kind, she said, she was safeguarding her territory. 'If I run out or send my people over to you, I'll lose them.'

To see me running from house to house, in the dark of night, borrowing five rand from this person, ten from that one and a whole twenty from another, you would have thought that I faced eviction for non-payment of rent or some other disaster of equal dimensions. During all this time, my benefactor waited, warning me each time I came back to report on the progress I was making: 'If you can't get the money, it is your loss. Don't ever say I never offered you a good deal, my friend.'

Finally, after many rejections, rebuffs and blunt refusals, I had the fifty rand. I had also discovered who my true friends were. There were some I had counted among friends but now knew to be nothing of the sort. As our people say, 'It is on a stormy day that the hen's tail is revealed' – *isisila senkukhu sibonwa mhla liqguthayo?* I was glad of the revelation. From now on, I sure would know who my friends were. And leading all the rest was my new friend, my guardian angel, the one person who was truly helping me by ensuring the survival of myself and my children. A truer friend I couldn't pray for. Five hundred rand! In my entire life I had never seen so much money. I was in a dizzy spin just thinking about it, about what I would do now that I was about to be rich.

It soon became clear to me that if I wanted that five hundred rand I would have to take my friend and benefactor to court.

True to her word, she came to get some of the marijuana from me. 'I'm sold out,' she whispered; 'now give me a parcel and let me sell that for you.' Thus did I part company with the first parcel. There were ten in all and each was supposed to bring me fifty rand.

In ones and twos the parcels left me ... though always without any money coming into my hands. 'They pay me at the end of the month.' And seeing my worry furrows deepening, 'Don't worry. I know them. They're good customers.' The parcels left me, and I was eager that they did. If I had not been in such dire straits, I'd have paid my friend to take the stuff. I could not sleep at night. Each footfall I heard was a detective coming to take me to jail. The morning sun ushered in a new set of fears. What if someone came to see me and innocently stumbled on my secret? I could smell the stuff the minute I walked in through the door. Were others so bereft of a sense of smell that they would miss that distinctive pungent scent?

Days became weeks and weeks became months and the months rolled on and still I waited for my money: at first the full five hundred rand, but as time passed I even prayed for the fifty rand I owed others who would not listen kindly to the story this woman was telling me. The customers she had so trusted were turning nasty and unreliable. 'Hanana hanana, my stallion has foaled. Hanana hanana, the uncle of my nephew's wife's sister-in-law's twin brother has lost a cousin of his mother's youngest uncle on her mother's side.' I could make neither head nor tail of her stories, but I gradually came to understand the sad fact that I would not see the promised five hundred rand ... not in a thousand years. I kept hoping to get my outlay back, the fifty rand for which I had scurried all over the place borrowing from women who made me grovel before they gave me their lousy fives and tens and other little bits and pieces. Surely she would give me that; I was certain. But, eventually, I knew I had to forget about even that.

Christmas 1966 found the elder of my brood, Thembeka Noluthando, ten days short of her fourth birthday. I was not planning a party. This was a time when each breath we drew was a celebration, so tenuous was our hold on life.

In the late afternoon of 24 December 1966, someone must have come to pay a sizeable debt. I suddenly found myself flush. I had an extra two rand.

Without delay, I hurried to Ackerman's store in Claremont to buy Thembeka her very first Christmas dress. I was afraid she might cry when, the next day, all her little friends would strut like courting peacocks, adorned in brand-new finery. I had discovered that by three, children can tell the difference between not just when they are scrubbed and when they are grubby, but between scrubbing that leads to church, scrubbing that leads to that most feared of people, the doctor, and scrubbing that promises the bliss of a fun-filled day.

Fortunately, we were saved from tears by this windfall and I reached the shop just before closing.

In the window I spied my golden treasure even before I walked into the shop. On a yellow background, a bold, cheerful, sunny yellow, danced blue, green and red polka dots big as five-cent pieces. Short sleeves, gathers at the waist, buttons down the back, two little belts at the sides to tie into a bow; the usual, run-of-the-mill dress for toddlers was, in my eyes, a gown fit for a princess. Down at an angle from right shoulder to left knee played a little frill of the same material and colour. The dress had been marked down from just under six rand to … ninety-nine cents.

I waltzed into the store on air. After some help from a saleslady (I didn't know the size I needed; when had I bought a dress for Thembeka?) I had a size six in my hand and fell in line behind others waiting to pay. My mind, how-ever, was miles and miles away. It was also hours ahead. Even as I gave the cashier one rand and received a cent from her I could see Thembi, gaily bedecked, tail a-wagging. She has always displayed the capacity to find joy and satis-faction in small things.

So we had a 'Happy, Happy Xmas!' Mother had found a pair of red sandals which my youngest sister Nomagqirha, then eight, had outgrown. Thembeka was as happy as happy can be. Thokozile, a year and eight months, was fobbed off with a dress of sky-blue with white trim whose origins I no longer recall. Once it had been washed and ironed, she, with all the fashion savvy of her twenty-month life, believed it was new. With a pair of brown shoes a neighbour's daughter had outgrown on her feet, Thoko paraded up and down N.Y. 74, the street where we lived, with a smile as wide as a doorway, all day long.

While the two girls preened themselves, went from house to house showing off their finery and receiving the custom-ary 'Christmas box' of food, sweets, and money, two-month-old Sandile demanded only that my breast frequently visit his voracious mouth.

On New Year's Day, friends, thinking to ease my pain, if for a day, took me to a stretch of beach set aside for Africans, Mnandi Beach. Of course, they had to pay my fare there and back. They had to feed me. I could make no contribution whatsoever. This they knew. What I doubt they realised was that they had to provide me with the clothes to wear – not just swimwear either. I had no clothes – dresses or shoes.

Someone provided the dress, on loan. And someone else stole her younger sister's shoes (not sandals) for me for the day. I felt terrible about the shoes because the owner, a gentle person, showed me such respect on account of my age and great education. Yes, I was a graduate of one of the finest teacher-training institutions of that time, St Matthew's Teacher Training College in the Ciskei.

The 'stolen' shoes, I still remember, were an ill-fitting, dark-brown, mean-looking pair of granny shoes, the kind that would, a decade later, become very fashionable. That day, these shoes served one purpose only: covering my feet during the trip to and from the beach. As soon as I got to Mnandi Beach I took them off and hid them till it was time to go home.

When Sindiswa, a friend and neighbour, had hinted that I come to the beach with her group, I had been reluctant. But Mother said she would mind the children for me and I should go, 'the sea air will do you a world of good'. A yearning almost sensuous stirred me to accept. I would go, I said, my mind's eye abandoning me where I stood trapped, as it leapt over miles to wave upon agitating wave of white-capped blue mounds.

Throughout the short trip, memories of happier days flooded my whole being. I remembered my childhood, a time of blissful ignorance. A time when I was unaware of so much that was wrong, evil even, with my world. Muizenberg had played an important role in that world; it had been 'the beach' then. When we talked of going to the beach, we meant Muizenberg. That was before the law told us to get out of all safe and beautiful beaches; that, in all the lovely stretch of Cape coast, we Africans were only allowed on Mnandi Beach. Uninviting. Unappetising. Bleak and desolate. Barren. And not safe.

But on that day the bleakness of Mnandi Beach was the furthest thing from my mind. Once more I was a little girl, today's cares a thing of a remote future I could not spy. Faster than the bus that took us there, I whizzed through time and lost myself in my idyllic past. Down the years I careered, away from the now. Lost. Lost. Lost to all care ... once more, that blithe spirit of yore.

Gaily, I splashed and frolicked, losing myself in the vast blueness, swallowing gulps of salty water, blinking as salt assaulted eyes, made skin tingly, awakening every cell. Then, all at once, panic.

My ring was slipping, leaving the finger it had guarded since my wedding day. In a blink, my fingers curled inward like lanky Muslims bowing in prayer. Somehow, thumb clamped the thin gold band to the last phalange of the finger it was fast escaping. Saved. Relief washed through me in a shiver from head to toe. Cold. Then I contemplated the meaning of the ring's narrow escape.

I had hardly had time to think before I caught the running ring. Alone I stood, ring clasped between thumb and ring finger – the other three, half bent, half straightened, looking on as if in witness to some solemn ceremony.

High above the fingers, my head woke up.

'What', I thought to myself, 'is the meaning of this ring? A symbol of love between husband and wife. Why am I wearing it, that love long fled?'

Then slowly, ever so slowly, fully did I open my hand. With my fingers relaxed, at ease, the ring swam away. And I, ringless, continued with my swim, now of more sombre mood without knowing exactly why.

Looking back, I now know that I had begun to 'let go'. I had embarked on the long journey that was to be the rest of my life, travelling light, sans husband. The act of letting the ring go was deliberate, but it was prompted, suggested if you will, by the workings of the waves. I am famous for hoarding, for stinginess and total inability to splurge even on myself. What possessed me then, that day, at that place, to commit an act of such reckless abandon?

I know I felt very satisfied with what I had done. To this day, I have not once regretted throwing the ring away. But I do not want to create the impression that I fully understood then the thorny path of single parenthood. It has been very much in retrospect (and with the very fortunate coincidences that have befallen me) that I have come to rejoice at being given a second chance to make what I would of my life.

Then, anger and even despair were perhaps what newly-husbandless I felt most of the time. But in the same way that the dry bean swells and its skin wrinkles and splits long before the new life that's about to burst forth is evident, even so I was pregnant with the me about to unfold.

On that first day of a brand new year, in my twenty-fourth year of life, in the agitating blue waters, I was born anew.

My physical birth had taken place in Gungululu in Transkei, a village near the little-known town of Tsolo, twelve miles from its better-known neighbour, Umtata. In a grey mud hut the colour of the earth from which it was made, on a bare, cow-dung-smeared floor, there my mother had squatted in answer to the primeval summons.

When I was four, nearly five, Father moved the family – wife and three children – to Cape Town where he worked as a labourer. And there we had lived, moving from one segregated residential area to another until, in 1960, we were moved (with thousands of other African families) to

Nyanga West, later named Guguletu.

Guguletu is a township. Up till this time, Africans in the urban areas of South Africa had lived in locations, in tin shacks that they themselves put up. Now we were being moved to townships: huge housing complexes the government built to house us. The government had decided on a slum clearance project. Well-knit communities were uprooted against their will and relocated to remote areas far from places of employment. Friends and families were scattered in the merciless dispersal. As vigorously as the government 'improved' our housing conditions, so was the fibre of community life rent, the glue that held us together dissipated. We paid dearly for our upgrading.

And what did we get in return? Bleak, same-looking matchboxes. Soulless and soul-destroying. Sub-standard. Uninspired. Hopelessly uninspiring.

It was there in Guguletu that a starry-eyed nineteen-year-old me began teaching. In 1962 I was a graduate of a two-year teacher-training course for which the prerequisite was Junior Certificate or tenth grade.

'Sindiwe, don't leave school. Finish high school. Do your matric.' This suggestion, bordering on lunacy in my opinion, came from Mrs Mbombo. Several years older and married with one child, she was a nursing sister. Later she would resume her own studies and become a medical doctor (one of probably less than ten female African doctors in the whole country at the time).

Of course, I scoffed at the idea. In mitigation, however, although I confess I felt highly educated, I also did not believe I had enough brains to pass matric. And I had irrefutable proof for such sound judgement.

Three almost grown men, who were anywhere between twenty-four and twenty-eight, had been wrestling unsuccessfully with matric for years. What dampened my aspirations to matriculate was the oft-repeated assertion: *'Bhut'* Mandla is bright!' This gentleman had failed matric four or five times.

'Sizwe is brilliant!' He should have completed a Bachelor's degree by the time he finally got his matric.

'Botha has brains!' He was still at it the last time I looked, twenty years after his first attempt. Okay, so he didn't study full-time, there may have been breaks in his studies also. But still.

And to me at that time, all men were infinitely brighter than women. Older people knew more. Therefore I condemned myself to never doing matric in the firm belief that if gentlemen of such superior age and intellect could not pass it, it was way, way above my own nothing-to-write-home-about mind.

I began teaching in April 1962, but I had to leave the profession six months later, pregnant. The next four years saw me get married, have two more children, work as a domestic servant, and lose a husband.

My husband had casually said one evening in June 1966:

'I'm going home to see my parents and I'll be back on the sixteenth of July.'

'Home' was more than a hundred miles away in one of the distant villages of the Transkei.

Not only did the sixteenth of July come and go, so did the sixteenth of August, of September, October, November and December.

The baby we were four months expecting when he left was born while he was still 'home'. He had done nothing at all about getting ready for the new arrival. Not a cent of his had gone to buying the baby's layette, paying for prenatal care, feeding me, the expectant mother, or feeding the two girls.

And now it was January. So, what with his six months of unexplained absence and the financial struggle during pregnancy, why should I have felt even a twinge of guilt that first day in 1967 as I abandoned the ring that a man who left me destitute had slipped on my finger, promising to love and cherish me 'till death us do part'?

The sixteenth of July became a big joke much later on in my life. I would say, 'Oh no, friend, don't you dare liken yourself to me. I will have you know I am a respectable woman. I am married and my husband will be back on the sixteenth of July'; and here I'd pause and, depending on what month of the year it was, watch people figure out how long it would be before this reunion. Then I'd set them free from their curiosity by adding, 'I don't know which year, though.' I would continue by explaining that even after I began dating again I made it a point that I was free every sixteenth day of July … 'In case it is *the* sixteenth of July', I'd say casually.

But I did not tell that joke the year freedom was thrust upon me. I did not tell it the next year or the one after that. For years I did not tell it. I was hurt. I was angry.

Yet, now I know it was exactly when I let that ring swim away, free, that I took the first healing step towards my own, me very own *free* state of being.

Six months and six days after I found myself a single parent, a new me emerged, the me who would one day laugh at the devastating event of being dumped by a husband. On the first day of a brand new year, in the cold, clear waters of the Indian Ocean, and with the grey-blue brooding mountains as midwives, I made my début.

Two

With an understanding the size of the point of a pin, I analysed my situation and arrived at a plan.

I was young and exceedingly foolish, and had a *mea culpa* personality. This last, no doubt, the result of my Anglican (Episcopalian) upbringing. Had it not been drummed into me when I was taking classes in preparation for confirmation that we, as individuals, must shoulder full responsibility for all facets of our lives, sin foremost?

To this day, I carry the indelible memory of the lay preacher who instructed me in the Catechism, Mr Ntenetya.

A tall, fleshy man, Mr Ntenetya wore his badge of Christianity visibly on his face, where it sat as brooding as the dark, quiet, heavy curtain that hides the sky before a summer storm. Only his big, luminous eyes sent signals: flashing with anger or dimming with irritability or long suffering or resignation. His weary bearing made it known that he, Christ's vassal, carried a heavy load in the shape of the rickety one-room tin shack we called church as well as the noodles who worshipped in it.

This gentleman came faithfully every Sunday, all the way from Langa, where he lived in a real house built of brick, a house with running water and electricity. We, his congregation, lived in houses not unlike our humble church, which, in all probability, was the sturdiest shack in Blouvlei – the name of the location where I grew up.

'Why does the Credo begin with the word "I" and not "we" although it was said by all twelve Apostles?'

This is one of those great truths Mr Ntenetya taught me:

'Each Apostle could only say what was in his own heart.'
Even to this day, I hear Mr Ntenetya intone.

I had learned the meaning of Personal Responsibility.
Learned it, never to forget it. Learned it to a fault ... often to
my own detriment.

Although I occasionally go to church and call myself a
Christian, even an Anglican, I would be lying if I referred to
myself as a 'practising' or 'active' Christian, to say nothing of
'devout'.

It was natural, given such clear teachings, that I readily
took the blame for the disastrous situation in which I found
myself. My understanding of my religion offered me little
solace. Indeed, by encouraging self-blame, it deprived me of
a sense of injustice ... of being the injured one.

The Church told me I was reaping the wages of my
labours. Society told me I was worthless because I was without a husband. The Department of Bantu Education, standing on high (if mythical) moral ground, rejected me as unworthy of serving its young wards whom it was energetically
stunting for all time. For four years I was not able to land a
teaching job, despite two principals who each asked me
twice to join their staff. Somewhere between my submitting
an application and the actual appointment something went
amiss. Not that I was ever told what that something was.

These attitudes found a more than willing victim in me,
one who fully participated in the reproach heaped upon
her. Had I not made my bed? It was very clear to me, therefore, that mine was to lie in it, thorns and all. I had learned
not to complain, and not to expect help from any source –
least of all the government. The only exception was perhaps
my family.

But the pay-off was that precisely because I could not
and did not blame others for the mess I found myself in, I
also realised and accepted that it was up to me to haul myself out of it. Because I expected nothing good from the
government, I did not wait for it to improve my lot. Indeed,

throughout my life, the government has never, not once, disappointed me. It has been singularly consistent in its persecution of the African, attacking the very foundation of our people – the family – robbing our young of a fighting chance to life, to dreams rightfully theirs both as members of the human race and as citizens of the twentieth century. No, if I was sure of anything, it was that I was on my own. If I was going to make anything of my life, I would do it without any help from the government, despite the government, despite the laws it had enacted and was, even then, enacting with the sole objective of our destruction.

It helped that my husband had done me the big favour of leaving me young. That, and the benefit of a childhood that had left me with a wondrously resilient sense of worth, were the strongest weapons in the war of survival I was about to wage.

My pride would not allow me to depend on my family. I had married my husband against my parents' wishes. Friends and relatives had advised me against the marriage. And he had known that. It seemed to me therefore that he owed me support and loyalty. Now that he had picked himself up and gone, how could I go to those same people who had seen me run eagerly towards this mess? How could I go to them and say: You were right and I was a fool? And have them tell me: We told you so. How?

I was still young, young enough to be naive, and my husband's leaving had made me mad enough to be vindictive. Moreover, the enormous mistakes I had made within such a short space of time had done little to cure me of the belief that my destiny lay in my own hands. I was even planning that of my children. My great plan of escape? My way out of poverty? Why, it was so simple: I would study that I might get a better job. That would enable me to educate my children.

My parents had raised me. Therefore, it seemed to me, I had the sole responsibility of raising my children. My husband's abandoning us made me more determined not to leave the children without father or mother. Indeed, it just didn't occur to me that this was an option.

Hard pressed though I was to give the children the most basic things, food and clothing, I had tremendous faith that I could turn things around. I am the mother of optimism.

I thanked God I had been left at that young age. 'Am I not lucky', I told myself, 'that he has left me now and not forty years later?'

It was clear to me that if a marriage was going to fail, the sooner it did so the better. 'How would I have been able to start all over again, an old woman, bent double, who had wasted all her life and the fruit of all her toil on a marriage that foundered and left her adrift with no anchor and no harbour to call home?' I asked myself, rejoicing at my great fortune: being abandoned while young.

I also tortured myself. The worm in my mind would not be stilled. What inherent flaw was lodged somewhere in my being? I asked, absolutely certain I was to blame for having chosen such a knave for a husband in the first place. How could I have been so blind? For years and years and years, the question pitted my soul.

Of course, the next step I should take was all too clear to me now. Eschew men, I told myself, basing that determination on two sound reasons: my apparent inability to judge a man's character and the equally apparent ability of men to change loyalty as a chameleon changes colour.

As *idikazi*, and one with three children to boot, I had added twenty years to my age as far as society was concerned. In the African tradition life is celebrated and children are treasured. It is ironic that women, the bearers of these national treasures, are at one and the same time praised for bringing forth babies and devalued for that very act. A woman is an old hag as soon as she has had a child. Anxious parents of young men warn their sons against dating such women. She has had a child, they say, therefore she is too old for you. And age is no asset until it is well-advanced, bent-at-waist, white-haired age.

The only men who showed any interest in me were of two kinds. If they were my age, they were far from serious. They would take my understanding of that fact for granted. We could be together, it didn't matter how long, but marriage would be out of the question. When time came for them to find wives, I should know and accept that they would be looking for young virgins, unspoilt and not saddled with children of their own. Older and very much married men were the other kind. However, added to my newly discovered distrust of men was a stubborn sense of my own worth ... difficult perhaps for others to see ... but undoubtedly there, firmly in place, with even the potential for 'great' prefixing it.

One of my anchors, my eldest brother Jongilizwe, had left the country. He was studying at Oxford University in faraway England. But I had inherited some of his friends. Among these was *Bhut'* Phakamile 'Paks' Masola, a leader at the Elukhanyisweni Community Centre which was right in front of my mother's house.

Paks's friendship was a godsend. Through him I met other men whose friendship was unencumbered with sexual overtures, rare in my time as a young woman. Zanemvula 'Zet' Zotwana is a friend from that time of my life. We were an informal, fluctuating group. Some were students at the University of Fort Hare and so were with us during vacations only. All were men except me, and all except *Bhut'* Sipho Malotana were bachelors.

I had always had a keen mind. In this group I used it, and I listened. At weekends, we would sit long into the night, engrossed in a discussion over 'the situation' or political trials under way or current affairs in the township or male–female relationships. These men took me seriously, liked and respected me. In fact, they often forgot I was a woman. I don't know if that was flattering, but at the time their acceptance of me as an equal was both a novelty and a balm. Paks, because of the closeness of his workplace to where I lived, became a brother to me. This group filled the void left by Jongi's being away and my decision not to have a lover. These men helped me more than they would ever know. All the bachelors had girlfriends and sometimes this complicated our lives, especially when the girlfriend was new and couldn't quite figure out where and how I fitted in the group. How I envied them their unquestioning faith in men, their unjaundiced view of human sexuality. I, veteran of the hard school of life, had vowed to stay away from the beasts. As friends they were fine. But never again would I put myself in a position where my happiness, my life, had anything to do with a man, I told myself … and meant it.

After weighing the situation, I had decided against taking my husband to court. And, as I was to see years later, that was a wise decision indeed.

The laws and regulations that govern every aspect of the lives of Africans make it almost impossible for African women to get redress when the man fails to support his children. Added to that, I am sorry to say, is the fact that African men, on the whole, regard giving money to wife or lover as payment for sexual and other services rendered. As soon as there is a breach in the relationship, the man stops giving the woman any money, irrespective of whether there are children born of such a relationship.

'She is sleeping with another man' will come from the lips of a father of five who cannot or will not see why he should give the woman, mother of his children, any money.

'Why should I feed another man?' he asks, bristling at such an outrageous expectation.

The questions the court would force the woman to answer are of such a personal nature and would be asked with such vulgarity and relish by a white man that I declined to give this satisfaction either to the black dog who had chosen to forget what had issued from his loins or to the white pig who would see not a woman or even a person but a bitch and treat me accordingly.

Instead, I struggled, stumbled and suffered – my eyes fixed on the reward that would be mine one day.

'They'll grow up,' I reiterated to myself, through clenched teeth. And believed what I said. I set my sights on the future, on a time when the children, grown up, well established in their lofty professions, would be on their own. And I could resume my life, have the young adulthood I had missed. Even then, I saw I had deprived myself of the care-free period enjoyed by those who finish school, find jobs, leave home, and enjoy life without hastily assuming roles of parenthood.

However, today made its demands. There was hardly time to court or nurse a relationship. There was firewood to collect from the forest where I chopped down dying branches of trees. With no cart or horse, I carried the bundles of wood on my head. There was fire to make. Outside. Sheep heads had to be seared clean of hair on the open fire. They had to be scrubbed, cleaned, cooked, and then sold. Money had to be collected from often slippery customers. Lacking capital, I talked the kindly butcher, the late Mr Njobe, into giving me credit. Five or six days a week, I took sheep heads from the butcher. I had done this from my fourth month of pregnancy when, unexpectedly, I found myself without a job and without a husband. Each head cost me twenty cents. And at the selling price of twice that amount, I was getting a hundred per cent profit. That is, on the days when I sold all the heads I had bought.

Often, though, that was not what happened. I lost profit to customers to whom I gave credit which they later did not honour. And some days I guess people just felt like something else. On days such as those, we did profit from being able to taste some of the sheep heads we saw daily but dared not eat. Unless, as I say, they threatened to go bad.

Relatives, friends, and even acquaintances advised my

parents to take me to 'someone' – a witchdoctor, who would surely take away the evil that denied me a teaching job. I was under a spell, couldn't they see that? 'Just look at her forehead,' said our would-be solicitous benefactors, alarmed.

I had a case of acne so stubborn I had come to accept its permanence. As it had come, so it would go, with neither help nor coercion from me, I decided. Just as stubborn as the acne, I resisted this remedy to my problem, although not from any lofty principle. As a child, I had succumbed to the ministrations of witchdoctors and medicine men. I had known no better at first, and when I did I was not freed from what I perceived as my parents' tyranny. They laid down the law, and their children followed it. After I had completed the teacher-training course, this problem had cropped up again. When at the start of the school year I had not been hired, my parents, with whom I was now living, hinted that I might benefit from going to 'one who sees', as traditional healers are sometimes called. I put my newly found professional foot firmly down. I had standards to maintain. I was educated, sophisticated and enlightened. How could I permit such regression?

But now? Now I refused to see a witchdoctor for a reason that had nothing to do with either principles or the elevated educational status that had done nothing to elevate me from drudgery and grinding poverty. Now naked fear was my motivation.

What if my ship was not seaworthy? What if it was rickety and leaked like a sieve? I was at the helm, or so I made myself believe. What was the alternative? Lying down and breathing my last?

Frantically, I turned to hospitals, hotels, restaurants and farms. Not even the lorries from the farms of Wolseley gave me a break. During the fruit seasons these lorries came to pick up labourers who were hired to help harvest the fruit. Lorryfuls of African men and women left the townships, and when some of these people returned, after absences that were sometimes as long as six weeks, we heard they had made money. No one said a lot. But then, no one we knew ever made a lot of money. We did not expect to, not in lives such as we lived. But fear drove me to a frenzy. I had to go on doing something even if it didn't amount to much. Any-. thing was better than admitting absolute failure, which going to the medicine man would have implied. Or worse, it would have been saying that a person or persons unknown had, for whatever reason, bewitched me and thence came all my misfortune: the children, the broken marriage, the un-employment and looming destitution. However, admitting that would have been far worse for me than enduring the difficulties with which I was faced.

I have this fear that if I ever believe that others wield power over my destiny, that I am so vulnerable, I might as well abdicate control of my life. For if I accept that, what is to stop me attributing to others (those who hate me enough to put a bad spell on me) all the setbacks I encounter? And once that happens, why would I do anything to get back on my own two feet? I would be virtually saying that it was be-yond me to reclaim myself. I would be accepting absolute lack of control. And the Good Lord knows, I had very little control over my life as it was.

This fear, this need to go on believing I am in the driver's seat, may be the one ingredient in my make-up I will not find it easy to relinquish.

Therefore, with everything that I cherished taken, broken or out of reach, I resolved I would become self-sufficient. I would work hard. I would study. I would pull myself up by my bootstraps. Yes, even though I had still to acquire the boots.

Three

The balance sheet would have made an accountant cringe. But I, no accountant, had my raw will on the credit side, and the experiences gleaned from the brief history of my life, experiences that were even then stamping themselves into the very core of my being:

> Ubohamb'uhamb'ubuye, bo!
> Abantwana bayalamba;
> Inkosikazi yakho, bo,
> Iphila nqokucela.
> Abakhelwana bayo, bo,
> Sebeth'ukuyibona:
> Bathi, khiyan'iminyango;
> Naku loku kuzocela!
> Bathi, khiyan'iminyango;
> Naku loku kuzocela!

Even today I cannot recall this song without my eyes smarting. That I didn't have a radio did not protect me from hearing it, over and over again as neighbours played their radios with the volume dial jammed up high. Those with record-players were worse. They would play the hit song of the time again and again and again as if they had no other record or were bent on playing it till it cracked.

The song, a lament about a forsaken wife and mother, accepts the fact of the husband's desertion, asks for his return, and cites as a reason: the children starve. The neighbours, on seeing the wife, say, 'Lock the doors, here's this coming to beg.' And a more apt description of my own position I could not imagine. Each time the haunting melody hit my ears, tears washed down my cheeks. Usually I'd be in the back yard scrubbing or cooking sheep heads or at some other chore when this happened.

Yes, it would be long months before I could earn my living less arduously.

The dominant feeling at that time of my life was a gnawing sense of shame. I was overwhelmed by a deep sense of shame that I had not lived up to expectations, others as well as mine.

By no means a wonder child, I had nonetheless been labelled clever. My parents, poor peasants, had paid for my education, for a Higher Primary Teacher's Certificate for Africans only, South Africa's third-class citizens.

I was subject to mood swings which, looking back, I find quite startling. Although, as I say, I wore the aspect of desolation, shifts to a lighter mood were not uncommon. And again, I found ample aids from the environment. With the ease of one who had taken psychedelic drugs I went from the one pole to the other, from desolation to, if not quite exhilaration, at least hope-filled tranquillity. Strangely, songs were my drugs. The lyrics of some were wings with which I flew from one world to another.

> It's just my funny way of laughing,
> Just my funny way of laughing,
> Your leaving didn't bother me.
> It's just my funny way of laughing,
> Just my funny way of laughing,
> I'm really happy as can be.

Whenever I was ready or felt the need to go over to a lighter mood, this song was my bridge. It reminded me that when my husband left we were definitely no longer in love with each other, that what his absence really meant was not the removal of affection but inadequate financial assistance. It helped me to laugh at him, at his great lack of insight, his inability to see into the far future when he would stand disgraced by the children he had not raised or provided with support. The song reminded me that I was far better off without him than having him remain in my life as a constant source of strife. Not unlike the whistling of a little boy alone in a forest at night, I needed all the crutches I could lay my hands on.

I set myself against the folly of loving another man by using the words of yet another song: 'Love to me is a misery. Love to me is a misery, loving you the way I do.' I fastened my heart on the 'misery', reminding myself that it seemed to be the only thing one could count on from loving a man. Misery. And I challenged myself to see as anything but misery having three children by age twenty-three, having to raise them by myself, with scorn and condemnation poured on my head.

Over and over again, I told myself that one thing and only one thing deserved my attention, and that was not a man. I reminded myself that I, with an education, something accepted by all as a ticket out of poverty, had managed to sink deeper into the poverty I was armed to escape than my uneducated parents had ever done. Gritting my teeth, I dreamt of a day when I would not only be proud once more of myself but would make all those significant in my life proud of me. Again.

Not my will, however, but a neighbour came to my rescue.

One afternoon, late in March 1967, the sound of children galloping came to an abrupt halt outside our door. We heard a knock, as timid and soft as the footsteps had been bold and boisterous.

'Come in, child,' said Mother, for the knocker's age was well advertised in both the reticent knock and the gait, full of abandon, that had preceded it.

A girl of about six stepped in. Breathless, she greeted us, and when we asked her what message she brought, she replied: 'Mother wants to know whether *Sis'* Sindi is home.' The words came out in hurried, husky puffs – in tempo, matching the footsteps of seconds before but subdued in tone (to go with the arena – indoors and grown-ups). Children have a perfect feel for theatre.

'Mother', whom I called *Sis'* Thandi, was a neighbour from down the road.

'Tell *Sis'* Thandi I am home but I can't come over today. If she wants me to plait her hair, tell her that will have to wait for tomorrow. I'm busy today.'

The child said she'd tell her mother and bounded away.

Sis' Thandi is Nomthandazo Beyi née Mtshobile. The prefix means she is older than me – which could mean anything from one year to ten years or more. She and her husband and their six or seven children lived around the bend from Mother's house, on the same street. She was the first person I knew as a child who attended boarding-school. She had completed Junior Certificate and a two-year teacher-training course. With the passing of the years, she has continued to dazzle me.

Two or three years before this, her husband had lost his driver's job. *Sis'* Thandi had stopped teaching after her marriage and was raising the children – four then and all under ten years, I believe.

Mother had been one of the people to whom *Sis'* Thandi would often send a child with a dish or a cup or a bag to be filled: 'Mother says could you please let her have some samp and beans for we have nothing to cook.' After some time, she had brushed up her old teacher's certificate, went out and got herself a teaching job. And although her husband later found himself another job, she had stayed in hers at Moshesh Higher Primary School in Langa.

This day, she must have been waiting for the child at the gate, for the child's footsteps were still in our ears when up the *stoep* came a *klop-klop, klop-klop,* followed by a high-pitched voice we knew well:

'*Kukho abantu nje kule ndlu? Nkqo-nkqo!* – Are there people in this house? Knock-knock!' she said, coming right inside the house without waiting for a 'Come in'. A grin as wide as the Sahara had painted itself on her face.

As we exchanged greetings and asked questions regarding the health of our respective families, she was as skittish as a young girl whose secret suitor has said he'd soon send word of his intentions to her father.

Then *Sis'* Thandi shouted to Mother, who was in one of the other rooms, '*Makhulu! Makhulu!* Please come and listen!' Mother appeared at the door between the dining-room and the kitchen, and they greeted each other smiling.

'I've come to take this girl back to where she belongs!' screamed *Sis'* Thandi, obviously happy at the news she had come with, at the joy she was bringing.

I sat there, too stunned to say anything, not willing to believe what I thought she was saying. Too scared to think such could be my luck that day.

'What are you saying, my child?' asked Mother, whose hearing was perfectly normal. Obviously, she too had difficulty digesting such unexpected good news, so needed and for so long elusive.

'There are two vacancies at the school where I teach. Sindiwe will get one,' *Sis'* Thandi replied. 'Here, I brought the application forms,' she added to my utter stupefaction.

I sat there as numb as though I'd been given an overdose of sedatives.

By sheer superhuman effort Mother managed to drag me back.

'Sindiwe, my child, God has finally heard our prayers. Do you hear what this child has come to say?'

Turning to Thandi, Mother said in a hushed voice, a voice I associate with the women's *Manyano*:

'My daughter, it is the witch who denies human increase. *Ukwanda kwaliwa ngumthakathi.*'

Any praise from my mother is high praise indeed. Mother, certainly to judge from the words that frequently spew from her mouth, lives by the words from a hymn that go '*ugqob-*

hoko olululo asinto ixelwa ngomlomo. Lubonwa nqezenzo' –
which loosely translates: True faith is not something announced by words. It is seen through actions.

And the words I had just heard come from Mother now
were words of high praise from any lips. Witches stand for
all that is evil, including taking away life. To my knowledge,
nothing is more valuable to us than the ability to bear children. Nothing is more cherished than a new person, as we
call babies. Even the Xhosa word for child, *umntwana*, a
little person, supports this.

And so, to say of someone that she is the antithesis of a
witch, is to attribute to that person almost godlike purity and
power. A fitting tribute, under the circumstances.

Thandi thanked Mother for her thanks and blessings.
Then she chirped, 'Let's fill in the forms. Do you know
where your certificate is?'

I didn't. My certificate, the legal document, proof of my
teaching proficiency, had by this time become more of an
embarrassment than an asset. Four long years I had labour-
ed in white women's homes, a domestic servant. I could not
get a teaching job because I was not a breadwinner. I had a
husband. Unmarried women teachers enjoyed preferential
hiring. That my husband had not earned enough to win any
bread cut no ice. Society insisted on regarding him, as all
others like him, as the breadwinner in our family.

The term for people like us is *the working poor*. It is a fitting term, a term I could have coined myself, had I not been
so busy living it. I did not know the term then. Neither did I
know I was in that category. All I knew was a burning
anger: slow, bitter, simmering in my throat and boiling out
into my mouth.

How unfair, I thought, that I had gone to all the trouble
I'd been through trying to be something when, apparently,
that did not matter one jot in the end. I had stayed in school
long enough to be something; my parents scraped together
enough to help me become something, but all I was

allowed to be was wife to my husband.

Again, Mother came to the rescue. While we completed the forms she ransacked her bedroom where all important family documents were kept in safety.

Mother is the repository of the family's history. She acquires papers, she is given papers by those who acquire other people's documents, and on rare occasions she is asked, 'Please keep this for me, Mama.' And although she'll bark back, 'Where do you see my safe in this house? Don't you have a suitcase just like me?', she'll take whatever it is she's being given for safe-keeping. And although her bedroom looks like the 'Lost and Found' department of some railway station, she is able to locate articles when they are needed.

My teacher's certificate was needed now. Thandi and I had not finished completing the forms when, with joy and triumph unmistakable in her voice, Mother said:

'Here it is!' And with a flourish, she plonked a frayed, light-brown envelope on the table. If I didn't get the job, it would not be because she had failed to do *her* job – to help me all she could. That's Mother for you. Ever prepared.

Early next morning I set off for Langa, about five kilometres away from Guguletu and about half an hour away by bus.

Although it was the March–April ten-day school vacation, Mr Malusi, the Secretary of the Langa School Board, was in his office. I knocked and opened the door to his 'Come in!'

Mr Malusi was as tall as I am short. Very tall. Moreover, his height was accentuated by the extraordinary litheness of his body. Not one ounce of fat, I'm sure, had ever inveigled itself into it. His head was small, his hair very short, so that the bald front patch was barely discernible. His lean, clean face housed sharp features: small, probing, beady eyes; a small pointed nose; tiny shell-like ears; a small thin-lipped mouth above which stood a thin, small, well-manicured, jet-black moustache that contrasted sharply with the small, curved, ivory teeth that peeped and hid as he talked.

I had seen Mr Malusi, I think, only once before the day on which I took in my application form. That was in June 1961 when, as a final-year student at the teacher-training college, I had come to submit my application for a post to commence at the beginning of the following school year. I had not heard from him since.

The Board was meeting that very evening, Mr Malusi informed me. He also wanted to know whether I was in a position to assume duties at the beginning of the next school quarter, in a week's time.

'Yes, Sir, I am free to start,' I said excitedly. Perhaps a wee bit too excited for Mr Malusi's comfort. He did not want any misunderstanding. And to make sure I did not leave under the impression he had promised me anything, he pounced:

'I am not saying the post is yours. The Board makes the appointments.'

'Yes, of course, I know that', I mumbled. I felt two inches shorter. He must have seen me shrinking because, flashing the only smile I spied during the whole interview, he added:

'I will know tomorrow morning.' He then asked me whether I was on the phone, saying he could phone me, or I would have to come to the office the next morning.

That is how my chameleonic luck suddenly and unexpectedly took on a brighter hue. My husband Luthando had been gone ten months. Sandile, the baby I was expecting when he left, was six months old. I was hired. I had a job, a teaching job!

The ease with which I regained professional respectability left me so opened-mouthed, any fly could have waltzed in and out at will. I was so astounded at the stupendous feat Mrs Beyi had performed to my gain.

Had it not been for her intercession, my uncertain application would not have gone forward. And as the teaching posts were not advertised, and I had become a little discouraged, I would not even have known of the vacancies at the school.

Two unmarried teachers were 'in the family way', so they had to resign their posts.

I tried but failed to see some hidden justice in my good fortune being tied to another's pregnancy. After all, even in my state of elation, there was no way the woman whose job I was getting could be tied to my own pregnancy that had resulted in my losing my job.

But that was almost five years ago. Now, new and pressing problems were at play. These were triggered by my unexpected change of fortune: I needed clothes. I needed travel fare. I needed someone to mind the three children. Practical, no-nonsense and crippling problems, they would become chronic with time. But that, I did not know then. Right then, all I saw was my golden gateway to financial security and social acceptance. My long waiting out in the cold seemed soon to be a thing of the past.

Another lesson I was yet to learn was the way few things happen by accident or in a straight and simple way. Getting a job, I used to think, was a simple matter of applying and, if you were suitable and the ablest of those who had applied, you happened to get the job. It would not be long before I knew how erroneous that belief was.

During my four year 'sabbatical' I had barely managed to keep body and soul together. The kind of work I had done while unemployable by the Department of Bantu Education was the kind that breaks the body and crushes the spirit. And that is what I had fought for four years to keep together, a bruised spirit and a spent body.

Not that I had much to show for it. Otherwise, I would not have been in such a financial dilemma. And, as I have heard said, *'Geld wat stom is, maak reg wat krom is'* – 'Money which is dumb makes right that which is crooked'. How then to straighten my twisted life without it? Once more, another woman came to the rescue.

Anne Mayne, classified white, is one of several friends I inherited from my beloved brother Jongi when he left the country to go to Oxford.

'Come to the flat and let's see what I can do,' Anne said, excited that I was to have a good job at last.

I returned from her place with a coat and two suits – one that I remember to this day, dark green with a subtle check. It had a cropped jacket that barely grazed the waist and the skirt had four box pleats, two at the front and two at the back, below the knee. There were also two dresses: my favourite, from Stuttafords, had buttons down the front ... all the way down. Brown, it had alternate dark and lighter stripes, three-quarter sleeves with upturned cuffs, a collar and matching belt. It was tailored, it was smart and I felt elegant wearing it. Elegant and filled with confidence. Also, Anne had given me two skirts, four blouses, underwear, stockings, and a pair of shoes. How lucky that we were only two sizes apart in dress size and a perfect match in shoe size. I had clothes to wear to work!

Anne, a little more conversant with the lives of her dark-skinned sisters than most whites in South Africa, knew, as I did, that I would not get paid until (with luck) the end of the quarter (three months' time).

Anne 'advanced' me some money monthly until I was paid.

Clad and with money to get to work, I would deal with the child-caretaking problem on a day-to-day basis, as I did with the unpredictable weather of the Cape summer.

Four

Restored, affirmed, encouraged, I grew hope sturdier than the giant yellowwood trees of the Tsitsikamma Forest. My heart, eternal optimist, was as fertile as the soil where these majestic trees thrive. And just as the yellowwood tree grows from the tiniest, most vulnerable plant despite trampling elephants, strangling vines and other threats, so did my spirits soar.

I have a job, a teaching job.
I have a job, a professional job.
I am restored to my rightful place.
I am restored. I'm whole again.

Thus joyously did my heart sing each day. Each day, though, I faced the problem of finding someone to mind my children, what food to leave them, how to get to work and back, what to wear. Practical problems. Landing a teaching job was the first step out of penury. However, it brought to focus a whole range of problems inherent in the very position of African women in the pecking order. The most pressing of these is certainly that of child-minding. African women, themselves hopelessly disadvantaged and the poorest of workers, cannot afford paid child-minders, and so depend on older children or on each other for this most important of functions. This requires goodwill from others and such skill in interpersonal relationships as would dazzle an experienced social worker.

Naturally, the first person I could turn to was Mother. However, having raised three younger daughters, she was anxious not to let them think that mindless breeding was acceptable in our family. There is a strong belief that if the eldest daughter in a family goes astray, all the younger daughters will follow her bad example. Certainly, I was no example any mother would wish her daughters to emulate. My mother was as keen as the next mother to raise daughters who would make her proud. Indeed, she was keener now. As a result of the mess I had made of my own life, she had to prove to the world that she was capable of raising good daughters. Mother must have decided that my lone struggle with my children would deter my three sisters from following my terrible example.

Exalted as she was that I was back in a teaching job, Mother let me know she was not minding my children.

Oh, if I was really stuck and it looked like I would have to stay at home, she would offer to help. But with that offer came much grumbling. She would take the children saying: 'Thembani, my baby, goes to school.' And, 'I do not want to change nappies anymore. God has not made a mistake. I have stopped having children because He knows I no longer have the strength to pick up wide-mouthed, screaming brats!' No, my sisters could not mistake the grudging nature of the help I sometimes received from Mother. They would be fools to follow in my footsteps.

Baby-sitting arrangements, therefore, became a rickety affair that depended a lot on Mother's mood each morning. I recall mornings when, as I opened the door to leave, she would announce: 'I am going to so-and-so today. Take your children to someone else.' Mrs Dinah Peters, the aunt of my sister-in-law, Jongi's wife, became a regular stand-by for such emergencies.

Baby-sitting in African townships is nothing like the intimate affair that exists in white homes. In the townships, children play in informal groups outside their homes the whole day long. They come indoors only when they are hungry or when summoned to come and perform some task such as washing dishes, sweeping and making tea, or when inclement weather forces every living creature indoors. The obvious exceptions of course are infants and toddlers still in nappies. My two girls would be mostly outside, but I still needed to feel that someone, an adult, would oversee them and take action should something happen. Sandile, a baby, needed more attention.

My situation was difficult but not disastrous. A lot of women, for ˙a variety of reasons, are not in employment even as domestic workers. Those women, my neighbours, became my stand-by child-minders. I trusted them in cases of emergency when it seemed the children would have to be left to their own devices or I would have to skip school. I would barge in at some poor woman's house on my way to work, children in tow, and say: 'Please help. Are you going anywhere or can I leave the baby here today?' If she agreed to mind Sandile, I would also leave the girls' food with her. Of course, come month end, I would remember these women, either with some groceries or with cash. There was no charge made for this neighbourly act. However, as we say, *'Isandla sihlamba esisihlambayo.* A hand washes that which washes it.' Religiously, I kept these hands clean, for they washed me and did so in a valuable and useful manner. And washed me almost daily.

These problems notwithstanding, like an alcoholic after falling from a wagon during a spell of enforced abstinence I was eager to prove my worth. Anne Mayne's generosity aided greatly in my ability to find baby-sitters. Money will turn the coldest heart to a cooing dove's. I learnt this as I was making my mark at Moshesh Higher Primary School – probably the most eager beaver the principal had ever seen in his life.

The principal, the late Mr Tabane, welcomed me with a slow smile, piercing look and firm handshake. I had never seen him before the day I presented myself as the newest member of his staff.

Blinded by my own happiness, I totally missed the frost

on his brow. The mechanical steps we went through were to me a warm welcome. Only as I observed him interact with the other teachers, and especially with the other new teacher, did I begin to see that something was amiss. That he was civil towards me, very civil, and warm towards others. That he had given me a handshake where he had given the other new teacher, Mrs Rozani, a hug. But I either brushed aside these misgivings or found reasons for them, impatient with myself for seeing slight where there was probably none. Sindiwe, I told myself, don't be childish now.

As days became weeks and weeks months, however, two things happened. I became convinced that the principal did not like me. When I confided this to my friend and bene-factor, Thandi replied: 'Don't worry yourself about that. He had his own candidate for this post you got, but the Secre-tary of the School Board owed me one.'

Simpleton that I was, it had not occurred to me that my own capabilities might have had little to do with my getting the job. Now that I was in the job, those same capabilities were taxed to the limit. Employers do not know what they lose when they overlook the desperate workseeker. With the explosive energy with which I had scrubbed sheep heads, I hurled myself into this job, and the similarity be-tween the two was not lost on me: I was still dealing with heads, some as stubborn to 'cure' as the blood-caked wool had been.

It was in my second year at this school that Mr Tabane said to me one day:

'I must confess, Mistress, I was very worried when you came here. There you were, no one from nowhere. Nobody had ever heard of you, and you landed on my lap. I had to conclude there was something between you and someone on the Committee.'

Seeing my look of utter astonishment, he went on: 'Mis-tress, put yourself in my position. How would you feel, knowing a member of your staff had the ear of the authorities?' I had to admit he had a point. My point was that I knew not one member of the Langa School Committee, except the Secretary, Mr Malusi.

Meanwhile, as Mr Tabane and I got to know each other, I became equally convinced that, despite his feelings about me, he was impressed with my performance.

If my memory serves me correctly, there were eight teachers, including the principal, at Moshesh Higher Primary School. There were two Standard Three teachers – Mrs Rozani and I; two Standard Four teachers – Mrs Beyi and Miss Mnyengeza; Mr Base and Mr Mehlomakhulu, the vice-principal, taught the senior class, Standard Six; whilst the principal and the youngest teacher on the staff, a man by the name of Mr Bruce Mbanga, taught Standard Five.

As *Sis'* Thandi Beyi and I travelled to and from Langa together each day, we soon graduated from being acquaintances of long standing to firm friends. Soon the prefix *Sis'* or *Sisi* before her name disappeared. It is amazing how eight (or even ten) years of difference in age means so much less the older one becomes.

Moreover, we both coached the netball teams. And, for me, that was to be the gateway to Mr Tabane's heart. Thandi was a good netball coach, but I was a fanatic as far as the game was concerned. I was also not above going onto the field as one of the players.

And we had good players who, with little training, would have become very good. We showered them with praise. We infected them with our own enthusiasm. We pushed them to their limits and beyond. In no time at all, we had a team that made very good rival teams quake in their kits. The Langa High School Netball Team, then under that great fanatic in all things educational, the late Mr Vincent Qunta, got as good from our girls as they gave. Mr Tabane and I became colleagues. We held each other in mutual respect. And we were friends until the last time I saw him, in 1988, at his house near Moshesh H.P. School with his wife and their daughter-in-law.

In the classroom I did my best, unconsciously and with minimum exertion. Teaching was still such a brand new thing of wonderment to me then that I truly revelled in it. My brief teaching job, back in 1962, had been with a Standard Three class. Now, nearly five years later, I was again teaching Standard Three.

Although the training I received at St Matthew's Teacher Training College was most probably the best of its kind available then, the very best training was given me in the primary school I'd attended as a child, where the teacher–pupil ratio had been, by Standard Six, the most senior class, one to eighteen. Granted, in the lower classes it had been less favourable. But still, it was nowhere near the nightmarish numbers teachers in African schools deal with today (or thirty years ago when I first taught there).

At the Retreat Presbyterian Primary School not only were the teachers in general good but a few were outstanding. The late Miss Edith Vuyelwa Mabija, Mr Magingxa and Mr Hobongwana come to mind, also Miss Sophetha, who later married and became Mrs Mgobozi. Perhaps because I kept in contact with her till she died and also because I had her as a teacher for two years running, Miss Mabija heads my list of what I consider to have been truly outstanding mentors, teachers through whose hands it is a blessing to have gone.

My own teaching, no doubt but a pale shadow of what these magnificent giants represented, was greatly influenced by this remarkable quartet. From the one I received stern discipline. The other showed me how that discipline could be tempered with sympathy and understanding. Another gave me the gift of love for books. And yet another, innovation and daring. Such were the talents I brought with me to Moshesh Higher Primary School. But there were glaring shortcomings too.

Teaching at primary-school level means teaching one's

class every subject in the curriculum. Of the three languages – English, Afrikaans, and Xhosa – I should only have been allowed to teach English. Xhosa grammar mystified me then no end. Afrikaans I knew almost nothing of, neither grammar nor pronunciation, and definitely not enough of the language to teach to anyone else.

My difficulties were by no means confined to the languages. History I knew something about, liked, and taught with reasonable confidence. Geography was another story altogether, a story of uncharted seas. But even this was nothing compared to the paucity of my knowledge of Scripture and the holes in what I knew of Needlework. I was expected to teach them to my class, and so I did, but at a cost.

The pupils must have sensed my nervousness and uncertainty and, perhaps without knowing why, found themselves uneasy in these subjects. I firmly believe that just as enthusiasm and confidence is transferred alongside whatever subject pupils learn, so too doubt and lack of comprehension are conveyed and assimilated. I would be very surprised if any of the pupils I taught Needlework became seamstresses or dressmakers, or if any of those I taught Religious Instruction became instructors, scholars, or ministers of religion.

Before I taught a new section of Religious Instruction or a new stitch in Needlework, I went for lessons myself. Mrs Rozani, a Dutch Reformed Church minister's wife, who had received instruction in Biblical Knowledge as befits the wife of a *dominee*, was of great help to me, enlightening me on this mysterious subject. As for Needlework, Thandi and I were often in stitches, late at night, in her house. The picture is vivid in my mind. There we sit by the table, hunched over some piece of material. She is attempting the nigh-impossible, teaching me the 'French seam' or making 'gathers'. Completely unable to grasp the measureless intricacies that transform a piece of cloth into a wearable garment with shape, I feel like an oversized crab which some cruel dance instructor is bent on turning into a performing star. God made crabs in such a way that they can't even crawl in a straight line. My inadequate education was forcing me to pass on a legacy of inadequacy to the next generation, my pupils.

1967. That was a year of transformation for me. I started teaching at Moshesh in April. But I did not get paid till the end of September. That was just one of the quirks of the Department of Bantu Education. It took them for ever to process information, especially that dealing with new teachers and their remuneration.

With my first cheque, I attended to essentials. I opened my very first bank account. This was a significant step in my development. In fact, this was a first not just for me but for my entire family. Mother and Father had never been inside a bank before.

I gave some money to my parents, perhaps the bulk of the cheque, because they had housed me and my children and fed us even when I had not given a cent to the common fund. Until this point in my life, they had given money to me; what little money I earned previously I had given them and they then decided how much of it would be for my personal use. This time I kept mine and gave over to them something to use any way they pleased.

However, it was not the amount of money I put into the bank that was significant. It was the act itself. It said: I am grown up. I am an adult who conducts her financial affairs on her own. I am independent. And my tomorrow matters. I think about it.

The fat cheque I got at the end of the third school quarter did not dazzle me at all. In fact, the reverse was true. It reminded me of the mean years, out in the cold, when I could not get a teaching position. The legacy of those four years drove roots deep in the core of my soul, left scars that refuse to heal and disappear despite all assurances and all evidence that I am not in want.

Five years before, I had been confident, sure I was a success in the making. Now I was sure of only one thing – I could never again be sure of anything good happening to me. My sense of security had been whittled away. I knew now that poverty is no respecter of educational qualifications. The rest of my life I have spent dodging Poverty's blows – real or imaginary. The fear that prompts the dodging is real. It is painful. It is stubborn and refuses to go away and leave me alone. Since that period of my life, when I had no certainty when my next meal would be, what it would be, who would provide it, my basic trust in things going well has fled.

Subtle changes were afoot. In the five years since I had left school, attitudes towards higher education were slowly changing in the wider society. More and more African students, young people, thought of it as something accessible. The mood of the 1960s filtered through even to us in dribs and drabs, but filter it did.

One day, returning from school, I bumped into Maggie Makhoba, then a student at the Langa High School. Maggie had been the youngest (and brightest) pupil in my class at Hlengisa Higher Primary School. As we chatted, she told me she was planning on completing high school before deciding what career to pursue – teaching or nursing.

By the time we parted company, the plan that had been hatching in my brain had taken distinct shape. If Maggie can do it, so can I, I told myself.

Clearly, Maggie's case reminded me of something I had forgotten: the cumulative nature of the education experience. I would study before I took examinations. I would rid myself of the fear that threatened to mummify me, the fear that matric was the moon before the Space Age and I was a village yokel who had not even seen a bicycle.

Even if I were so slow that I could pass only one subject a year, I asked myself, would I not have completed matric by now?

Yes, it was 1967, the sixth year after I had left the teacher-training college, full of myself, mesmerised by my own brilliance, confident the world was at my feet.

So in September 1967, I became a student of the Damelin Correspondence College, which is based in Johannesburg. When the first batch of lectures arrived by mail from Damelin I was beside myself. Anxious, excited and enthusiastic. I raced through the first booklets on each of the four subjects I had enrolled in, did the exercises and sent them off. Then, while I dug into the second set, I awaited the return of the corrected exercises with the eagerness of a bride of less than a week. The feedback, when it came, was encouraging and prompted me to work steadily at my studies.

By the end of the year, the fear of sliding back into destitution had given wings to my soaring hopes.

'Sindiwe Magona, matriculant!' became a familiar castles-in-the-air joke among friends and colleagues at Moshesh. But to me it was less of a joke and more an earnest reality.

Deliberately, I had counted the number of teachers at the thirteen or so higher primary schools in the Langa-Guguletu-Nyanga area who had matric. There were about two, both men.

Because I was married (I never did get a divorce), I could only be given annual contracts, temporary posts. Permanent posts were for real breadwinners – all men, irrespective of their marital status, and also unmarried women. I was not a breadwinner in the eyes of the Department of Bantu Education, my three children and their errant father notwithstanding.

And so I counted on the thin crop of teachers with matric to entrench myself in a teaching post. To compensate for the great sin of being married, I would become matriculated.

I began to joke that I would boast of my high qualifications one day. On meeting someone for the first time, as I extended my right hand in greeting, I would say, 'Sindiwe Magona, matriculant.' Those days, people still appended

B.A. or M.A. to their names. And since those dizzy heights were beyond my reach, 'matriculant' would more than suffice, I reckoned.

What was not a joke, as I got involved with my studies, was coping with the triple bind: single parenthood, work demands and ambition, even the mild ambition of wanting to complete high school. That ambition was greatly aided by the enticing, if misleading, advertisements, 'Get matric and doors will open for you!', used by some of the correspondence schools, advertisements which found a more than willing victim in gullible me.

'And a white skin.' Why had these same advertisements not included the one criterion that was crucial in getting a job? Even a cursory glance through the classified section of the newspapers would have told me that a white skin was what I needed most.

With such a frantic lifestyle, I soon learnt the art of juggling. Nothing short of a magician's skill and cunning could enable me to do everything I had to do, and by the end of 1967, facing the first year of formal studies, I had become an adept juggler.

I sneaked Thembeka into school although she was barely five years old. But I had the two younger children to worry about. And worry I did.

Keeping Thokozile clean became increasingly difficult. She was a tomboy even as a baby. With each passing week, her prowess became legendary. She got into scraps with the regularity of a shebeen queen. She got her clothes torn. She beat other children. She was more than I could handle.

Happily, Sandile would remain a baby for at least another two years. Little did I know how his growing would wreck my peace of mind.

My day began at five in the morning and ended at midnight. I left the house at six o'clock. By half past six I was at school. This gave me two and a half hours of study time, for school only started at half past eight.

More important was the school's electricity, which I didn't have in my house. Guguletu houses have neither electricity nor hot water. And the space! Space where I could have quiet. After school I would go home, do chores and take a nap till ten o'clock when everybody was asleep or at least in bed. Then I would get up and put in two hours of studying. My life was under rigorous reconstruction.

By the time I left Moshesh, I had gained the admiration of the principal for industriousness, punctuality and regularity. He had no way of knowing that the conditions under which I worked, compared with what I had already been through, seemed to me heaven-sent indeed.

For example, mindful of the reluctance of principals to have women with children on their staff, I never used mine as an excuse for either lateness or absence. If a child needed to go to the clinic, I found someone who wasn't working to take the child there. My mother and my neighbours were very helpful in that way. And when month end came, I would remember the favour with an extra chicken, packet of sugar, tea or coffee.

Indeed, the principal wasn't aware I had children until the middle of my second year at Moshesh. And that fact happened to slip out during a conversation when he challenged me saying, 'What do you know about children, Mistress? You have no children.'

'But I do have children, Sir! I have three,' I had replied smiling, much to his astonishment.

Drunk with my ability to discharge my duty – feed and clothe my children, take them to the doctor when necessary – it never occurred to me that what I was doing could have a negative impact on them. Sure, their father had upped and left us. But were they in want? More than they would have been with him around? Honestly, no … in my opinion. I was so busy being the breadwinner that I now know my children never had a mother. I was the head of the family. Their well-being depended on me. I worked. I dished out discipline. I created a place where they would grow up well mannered, purposeful. I was father to my children. I shunned those things mothers do, cooing over their children, providing them with the gentler side of parenting; I deliberately suppressed things like these. They petrified me no end. I believed if I showed the children tenderness they would get spoiled as there was no father to counteract with stern discipline. I was bent on raising children who would defy the stereotype of children raised by *idikazi*, a woman alone, a woman considered by consequence of that fact alone as morally bankrupt. No, my children never had a mother. In me they had a father.

It was as if I had blinked and missed a whole year. That is how the year swiftly sped away to disappear into the grey pages of memory. Before I knew, the end of the year had come, bringing with it the almost forgotten phenomenon – fear of examinations.

Only fear of the consequences forced me to sit for the exams. I had enrolled for four subjects, English, Xhosa, History and Biology, staying, as I thought, with subjects I knew something about. I shunned subjects that I thought exotic or difficult – Economics, Criminology and Mathematics – not realising I knew so little as to make no difference between the subjects I chose and a host of others I could have done.

Now, confronted with the enormous gaps, with ignorance so great even I knew I could not but fail, I made a very wise decision.

I remembered an episode from my Langa High School days. A grown woman, a teacher, had deferred entry into the workforce in favour of completing high school. So she was a student for two years ... doing matric. She'd passed the first year. At the end of the second year, when the exams arrived, she was far from ready. And she opted for not taking the exams.

Nearer home, I recalled how my own registering with

Damelin had enthused the principal and one of the male teachers into enrolling with a different correspondence college. A representative of the correspondence college had come to the school canvassing students from among the teachers. Mr Tabane and Mr X enrolled. This happy event took place during the morning, before lunch break.

After lunch that very same day, an irate Mrs X was in the principal's office. She had come to make the principal undo the contract her husband had signed earlier that day. *'Yimali yabantwana bam le adlala ngayo!* It is my children's money, this with which he plays.' Thus had the wife of this teacher expressed her disapproval of her husband's enrolment.

No. She was not anti-progress. She did not begrudge her husband's advancing himself through studying. She was just plain sceptical of his ability to do so. And in all fairness, she had a point for, as she remarked, 'Three years ago, the same thing happened. He paid all that money, and there are those books the school sent him gathering dust right under my bed.'

Apparently, both gentlemen had not only toyed with the idea of studying for matric, they had actually enrolled. But that was where their dreams had ended. This year, then, it was for both the second time they were enrolling to do matric.

I scared myself I would fall into the same pattern: marking time, doing the same course and never completing it. Stimulation, never fulfilment. Perpetual but fruitless studenthood. 'I will write,' I told myself. 'I will not take the easy way out.'

It seemed clear to me then that I had to experience the pain of failure and not avoid it. I had truly to feel the folly and fruit of not working consistently during the year.

So, hopelessly ill-prepared, in November–December 1968 I sat for the examinations – external examinations. Although I knew I had not prepared myself for the exams, suddenly, having written them, I felt I had a chance: a slim chance, but a chance nevertheless.

The actual examinations were a depressing surprise. I was surprised at how much I knew and depressed at the realisation that had I but applied myself, even a little harder, stretched myself a little more, I would have been assured of success.

Now, the agony of waiting gnawed at me – day and night, night and day. One minute, I would be very hopeful indeed. The next, down Despair Donga I would plunge.

Then on a Thursday in mid-January, I heard the results were out. One of the Anglican Mothers' Union women of my street sent a child with the news. That is how I know it was a Thursday. Anglican Mothers' Unions (as, indeed, women's groups of all the other denominations) meet on the Thursday afternoon.

My legs were wings as I raced down N.Y. 1, Guguletu's main street, hoping that a car would stop and give me a lift. In record time I was at the Anglican rectory where the priest, the invigilator during the exams, had the precious results of the private candidates.

To my timid knock, the Right Reverend Ndungane boomed a nasal, 'Come in! Come in!'

Reverend Ndungane, then of St Mary Magdelene, Guguletu, was a gentleman who, if he had ever known it, had forgotten the word 'hurry'. That is not to say he dawdled. No. He simply wore an air of deliberateness just as most people wear shoes. He walked with deliberateness. With great deliberateness, he talked, preached and smiled.

This day, he was not about to step out of character because of my anxiety.

Thus, with deliberateness, we greeted each other. Or rather I greeted, humbly as befits a worshipper, and he responded with great dignity as befits a man of his age and station. We inquired about each other's health and listened to each other's response with barely concealed boredom. I was dying inside. But I knew my place, and knew it well. The Reverend also knew my place, very well indeed. He was that kind of man.

At last, he asked, by way of telling me (deliberately):

'I suppose you have come to see the results?'

'Yes, *Mfundisi,*' I croaked.

'Do you think you passed? How many, by the way?'

'Four, Sir. I hope so, Sir.' Did the man have no heart? I thought fuming.

He must have sensed my growing alarm and perhaps feared I might come to harm and he would have to put himself out on my account: drive me home or offer some other help. He stood up and beckoned, leading me to his study.

I gave my surname, my maiden name. I had decided to simplify my life. All my certificates are in my maiden name. With my husband departed, I saw no reason to saddle myself with his name. Moreover, why would I want to work hard and then carry the laurels to a family that had not even paid lobola for me? Why would I thus grace and exalt his family name? I dropped his name and, once more, used my own, the familiar name I had so long loathed. MAGONA. How I loved it now.

No one was more surprised than I was: I had passed all four subjects. I, who had feared my brain had turned to sawdust, I had passed the examinations. All four subjects.

My joy was boundless. My faith in myself restored. I was so proud of myself that I was in real danger of bursting apart. The symbols, English – C, Xhosa – E, Biology – E, History – E, troubled me not in the least. I had passed. There my focus was. Passed.

My joy, unfortunately, was to be my ticket to a teaching post at a post-primary school, taking me away from Moshesh Higher Primary School and away from kindly Mr Tabane of the dimpled smiles and mischievously laughing eyes.

Five

A harsh reality dampened my pride. Like a witch's wand, it changed the sweet taste I savoured to gall. My achievements turned to dust. Because I was a married woman, I was condemned to a temporary post. And so at the end of each school year I, and other married women like me, became jobless and had to reapply for our positions amid stiff competition.

Every January, a new crop of recently graduated, fresh-faced anxious teachers, eager to enter the world of work, emerged to threaten the livelihood and job security of the old horses. Like me, the older women ran households. They were wives with demanding and often unappreciative husbands. They were fully participating members of the community: they belonged to church women's unions; they ran Girl Guide companies; they were members of the National Council of African Women; they organised themselves, formed street associations, burial associations, benefit societies and they ran these efficiently. They were members of the clans into which they were born, participated in the life of those clans, as well as in those of their mothers and the clans into which they married. But each January they were forced to re-enact the experience of entry into the world of work, to seek renewal of their contracts, which ensured they would return to the same school. Or to hope, in the event the renewal was not forthcoming, for a new contract, a job at another school.

The Department of Bantu Education saved itself a lot of money on the backs of married women. Each January, these women, once more re-employed, would not receive the full month's salary. As the school year usually began on or after the third week of the month, about three-quarters of a month's salary was thus saved. Moreover, since new employees usually received their salaries only six to nine months after the date of employment, the Department earned interest on these deferred salaries. The Department of Bantu Education has always had a problem as to where its loyalties should be: the people it purports to serve or the masters whose creation it is.

Thus it was that a week or so before schools reopened in 1969, I went to see Mr Victor Sipoyo. He was the Secretary of the Nyanga School Board. I was certain my contract would be renewed at Moshesh. But where was the harm in making doubly sure I would have a job on opening day? Just in case? My experience of the world of work had left me anxious, devoid of trust, fearful.

It was a clear early morning in January, the kind of day that ensures summer will be missed. No sooner had I walked into the office than Mr Sipoyo, beaming from ear to ear, hailed: 'Mistress! You are the very person I wanted to see today.'

I smiled as we exchanged season's greetings and took a seat. Mr Sipoyo continued: 'How did you know I wanted to see you today, Mistress?' I could give no definite answer to that, and to this day I do not know what prompted me to go to an office that had shown singular reluctance to employ me. Could I have been drunk from the heady news of having passed four matric subjects? That is a clear possibility, for in my eyes it was nothing short of a spectacular achievement. And a tremendous boost to my ego.

Another reason was that the Nyanga School Board had just had a change in personnel. Mr Sipoyo, I knew, was new in the post of Secretary. His predecessor was the gentleman who had found me completely and utterly unemployable.

But now, in 1969, the School Board was under new

management and I was not as desperate as I had for so long been. I had been teaching for almost two years and I had escaped from destitution. My status had changed to that of the working poor.

The reason Mr Sipoyo was anxious to see me, he said, was that the principal of the (then) only post-primary school in Guguletu, Fezeka Secondary (now Fezeka High School), wanted me to join his staff.

Why had Mr Sipoyo not contacted me before I came to see him? The answer was quite simple: the Secretary of the School Board had a phone but less than one-tenth of the teachers he serviced had phones in their homes. It was only in the late 1980s that it became an accepted practice to offer this service to Africans too. Before that, an African had to have special needs to be considered worthy of a telephone in his home.

Delicious disbelief churned in the pit of my stomach as I listened to Mr Sipoyo's words. It forced my mouth open, and I heard a stupid-sounding voice announce:

'No. Teach at a secondary school? Me? No, I couldn't.' Yes, that is what *I* said. Though my confidence had risen sky high, I was not so confident that I was ready to fly in the Apollo. Even in my elated mood, with a sense of my own importance growing by the day, scars of yesteryear still ran deep. And I would walk with the shadow of self-doubt for a very long time.

Mr Sipoyo was trying to convince me of two things while I, equally vehement, voiced disbelief and grave doubt about his proposal. Mr Ngambu, the principal of Fezeka Secondary School, had asked for me himself. He wanted me in his school and he, Mr Sipoyo, was confident that Mr Ngambu knew what he was doing. 'It is his decision and I am sure it is a good decision. You will cope well at Fezeka.'

'No!' I said again.

'Yes, Mistress,' said a voice from behind me. A firm voice, although the words were softly spoken.

I turned round and froze, looking straight into the eyes of the Principal of Fezeka Secondary. With my back to the door, I had not noticed Mr Ngambu walk in.

Mr Ngambu, a well-mannered, quietly spoken gentleman of great refinement, wore authority the way Royalty wear crowns. Even in 'civvies', the halo is there. I am sure, if one came across Mr Ngambu on his knees, gardening, one would somehow know he is a man with a great deal of authority.

Whereas I had been arguing with poor Mr Sipoyo, I was all acquiescence in Mr Ngambu's presence. Two or three sentences from him and I was ready to sign the forms requesting employment by the Nyanga School Board.

Of course, I still had to notify poor Mr Tabane, the principal at Moshesh Higher Primary, that I was no longer looking for renewal of my position at his school. I was leaving Moshesh, the school that had given me a foothold, and I had not even had the opportunity to bid adieu to the students or the teachers – another unsavoury side-effect of the temporary teaching posts married women are forced to accept.

The move to Fezeka was not without financial reward. I no longer had to worry about train-fare; I could walk to school. Moreover, there was another twist to the affair. I was qualified to teach at the higher-primary school level. Yet ironically, because I now taught at a secondary school, I enjoyed job security. Shortage of teachers qualified to teach at the post-primary school level made it possible for me to get a permanent position (although nothing had changed regarding my marital status). Moreover, I now received ten rand more per month. This was called the secondary post allowance.

I felt twice honoured to be a member of the staff at Fezeka. As the then principal would often boast: 'Fezeka! Be perfect!' And, for an African school in South Africa at that time, Fezeka was as perfect as perfect could be.

Mr Ngambu, the principal, wanted me to 'polish' the English of the intake class, Form 1. Straight from the primary schools that fed into Fezeka Secondary, the new Fezeka students presented an interesting phenomenon.

Given a topic, say 'A Visit To The Zoo' or some other subject of equal fascination, these one hundred and fifty students would hand in startlingly identical work: testimony to the hard work and zeal of the Standard Six teachers who had prepared them for the entrance examinations qualifying them for high school. From reading the essays, one could easily tell which students had come from the same school. And that was a tribute to the memorising ability of the students. Rote learning, even of whole essays, is still very much a part of what passes for education for Africans in South Africa to this day.

'Mistress,' Mr Ngambu pleaded, 'teach them to produce rather than reproduce. Let them learn how to express themselves.'

As I have mentioned, I had been not a little apprehensive in accepting the post at Fezeka, painfully aware of my lack of qualifications to teach there. There had to be a difference, I figured, between teaching primary school pupils (which I was trained to do) and teaching high school students. However, Mr Ngambu constantly assured me he would not have asked me had he not been confident I was equal to the task.

'I've been listening to you speak at SWATA meetings,' he often countered, allaying my anxiety. For once, my big mouth had served me well. Mr Ngambu's statement and the studies I was doing through Damelin Correspondence College gave me some measure of confidence in teaching at a secondary school.

And then my confidence received a boost from, of all unlikely sources, a panel inspection.

I had been at Fezeka less than three months when inspectors visited the school.

Although I have no recollection of a teacher actually getting fired because of a recommendation arising from a panel inspection, the dread with which teachers awaited it, however, led one to believe that this was the most common result of these inspections.

I doubt that there was a more nerve-wracked teacher at Fezeka as the panel inspection drew inexorably nearer and nearer. Nothing would have made me happier than falling ill and being forced to go on sick leave just then.

Perhaps precisely because of my insecurities about teaching higher classes than I had been trained for, I put a lot of effort into the preparation and teaching. More, perhaps, than I would otherwise have done. At the same time, the school had some funds and the principal was not only receptive to innovation but encouraged it. I bought books. I bought flash cards. I bought other teaching aids, and used them. I learnt to use the overhead projector – I, who had still to learn to use a stapler!

Moreover, as a spin-off from my own studying, I had a better grasp of the English language than when I had completed teacher-training. And I had not been bad then. I also began to frequent the public library (this was before the country took a leap back into its future and barred Africans from the city libraries), and read books on the teaching of English.

Creative writing was a brand new concept to me then. I found it not only exciting but exceedingly useful, helpful in combating overwork. Giving an essay to the students stopped being an exercise in self-torture. I learnt that an essay did not have to be any specific length. An essay, *mirabile dictu*, could be just the beginning or the ending of a story or a piece of composition. How exciting, practical and creative.

Soon, too soon for me, the week of panel inspection was upon us. Mr Stone, a white school inspector, was the member of the panel who evaluated the teaching of English. So it was he who came and sat in and watched me demonstrate my ability to teach the language to Form 1 students.

The students were nervous. I was nervous. The only two people in that classroom – where near to sixty people were crammed – who were not nervous were Mr Stone and the class clown.

In situations such as this, where I have no control whatsoever and am at the mercy of others, I have developed a *modus operandi*. To break the grip of fear, I tell myself that whatever the difficulty I am faced with, it will not kill me. And since I have no choice but to perform the task, I may as well give it my best. That is how I psyched myself through the awful exercise. I was convinced I would reveal my inaptitude, lay bare the fact that I was an impostor. 'Unfit to teach secondary school!' – I was petrified the inspectors would recommend.

Well, not only did I receive a flattering report but I was invited to give a demonstration lesson at a refresher course for senior English teachers. When I demurred, my Principal gently chided: 'But you must go, Mistress. This is a feather in the cap of the school.'

How could I disobey such an explicit order when Mr Ngambu himself pointed out my duty to me so clearly?

I did not recognise until now as I write that that was the highest, in fact the only, compliment I ever received from the Department of Bantu Education, my former employer. I am not saying I should have received more (or any for that matter). But yes, I must admit to the only regret I have about my job. I am sorry I no longer teach. I miss teaching; with all its frustrations, its pitfalls, its pitiful remuneration, it is still a great job, a challenge and rewarding. I liked it.

Long after I had left the employ of the Department of Bantu Education, I helped students at the primary-school level prepare for examinations. At first, these were mainly my siblings and their friends, the children of friends, relatives, neighbours and, later, my own children.

As these students progressed to high school so my

responsibility grew. Later still, in tandem with my own progress, I would tutor high school and university students.

I remember teaching a young man, white, member of NUSAS, who needed his Xhosa I in order to graduate at university. He was desperate. He had failed the subject and was none too sure of himself as the date of the supplementary examinations approached. We worked on his composition, both oral and written. We worked. And worked. And worked. He was not shy of work, but for some reason he had completely missed out on learning to order his thoughts and present them simply but well and convincingly in Xhosa. On the evening after his exams, he drove all the way from Sea Point, where he lived, to Guguletu, he was so excited at how comfortable he had been. 'The guy who gave me the oral was beaming at the end!' And when the results came out, YES, we had done it. I was so proud of myself that one would have thought the University of Cape Town had conferred the degree on *me.*

Another motif from my tutoring days that has stayed with me and amuses me to this day involves my youngest brother, Thembani, and Thembeka, my eldest child.

It must have been November or early December, for the two were writing the Junior Certificate exams. On this particular day, they had Xhosa Literature in the afternoon. I remember clearly, for it was late morning when they came to me, exasperation written all over their faces.

'*Sisi,* please help us with this book,' ventured Thembani whilst my daughter tried to be invisible, standing slightly back and behind her uncle. I had a simple rule about helping students with their school work: let us work on it together, through the course of the year preferably, or at least over a decent period of time. I didn't think it helped anybody very much if we sat up through one night and crammed the key points or tried to 'spot' likely questions. But what is principle when faced with one's first-born and one's youngest sibling? I succumbed and without grumbling, as they had left me with no time for that. The exam was in a matter of hours, and here they were telling me they had not the foggiest about a whole book, not just a chapter or the mystifying end.

The book in question was the great novel *Ingqumbo Yeminyanya (The Wrath of the Ancestors)* by the late A C Jordan. The book is a classic. As I workshopped it with the two, I got involved in its world, a world of intrigue, of a people caught up in a situation of confusion, of transition, of changing ways and resistance to that change. A world steeped in rich tradition but having to come to terms with in the inevitable passage of time and the painful uncertainties wrought by that.

By the time they had to go for the exam, *they* were telling me what a great story this was. They even had the good sense to express regret that we hadn't worked on it earlier, longer and more thoroughly. Not only had we examined the themes so eloquently presented in the book, we had covered its rich language, met the characters, travelled with them through their ups and downs.

Well, I am told that when someone is wearing a sparkling diamond a bit on the large side you can bet your bottom dollar the stone is a fake. From the thanks I got for my pains, I think the same principle applied in this case. I was just a bit too good to be true. I lost credibility that day.

'Well? How did it go? I asked, excitement I could not hide lacing every word, evident in my wide-open eyes.

Coolly, and in a voice suddenly grown up, my brother answered, 'You had seen the questions!' Thembeka was nodding concurrence, eyes looking at me, daring me to deny the accusation. I just stood there, utterly deflated.

Ingqumbo Yeminyanya is one of the few Xhosa books that people read for pleasure. I had read the book before I met it in school. In my teaching and in my tutoring, I had again dealt with it. I had a pretty good idea of the issues, themes, events, characters, language. I knew and loved the book. Tembani's scepticism was therefore an unkind cut and it was particularly painful for the disillusionment it revealed ... and in people so very young.

It was not for me I ached but for Thembeka. For Thembani. And for all the young people of my country, faced with times so uncertain, so filled with turmoil, so unpredictable and so untrustworthy.

Of course, I tried my best to correct their misconception. But I was up against a hard one. Unfortunately, this was the time of *intluva*, when access to examination papers became so widespread that students spent their time hunting for exam papers rather than preparing for the exams. I was not even teaching then. How could I have had any knowledge of the paper? But, then, how did students gain access to them? Given such anarchy, could I really blame Thembani and Thembeka for their lack of faith in me? Still, the accusation hurt.

It is this unpaid teaching, which was not recognised officially and for which no record exists except perhaps in the memory of a few, that I am proudest of. For the opportunity it represented, making a difference in the lives of other people, I am truly grateful. It is not often that one is called upon to add a stitch as people weave their dreams. I have been that blessed.

Fezeka Secondary School was run along the lines of mission boarding-schools. No doubt, the principal was a product of such a school, and so also for that matter the members of staff.

Until the sixties, most (if not all) African boarding-schools in South Africa were mission schools. All teacher-training schools were boarding-schools too. Certainly, this was the case in the Cape Province where all the teachers at Fezeka Secondary School would have received their training.

Discipline and industry were the twin pillars on which Fezeka was built. Throughout the school, from the principal to the students, from the teachers to the clerical staff and the caretaker and the cook, there was unity of purpose. The common aim, among the staff, was to impose the strictest measures of discipline on the students, and, among the students, to get an education in what was considered an excellent institution.

Such Spartan conditions, it was assumed, would foster good working conditions which, in turn, would encourage the students to lean towards industry and achievement.

There were incentives, too, for students who applied themselves. Foremost of these, the promise of cutting a year off the Junior Certificate course.

African students not only started school later than children of other race groups, they also had an extra year to go before they completed Junior Certificate or Junior High School. Again, I do not pretend to understand the workings of the minds that plan these things for Africans. Suffice it to say, it is the law that African children have to be admitted to the first year of school after their seventh birthday. To prevent any misunderstanding and ensure compliance, an earlier stipulation of seven years was later changed to 'eighty-four full months'.

Barring promotions, failures and other spectacular events of that kind, African youngsters were fourteen years old by the time they finished primary school, seventeen at the end of Junior Certificate, and, for the few who survived the obstacle course, nineteen when they left high school.

At Fezeka Secondary School, the three-year Junior Certificate course became a two-year course for the very bright student. At the end of the first quarter, exams were set and those Form I students who demonstrated exceptional ability were promoted to Form II. And most of these students went on to obtain a first-class pass the following year when they sat for the external Junior Certificate examinations.

Hand in hand with the discipline imposed on the students and the industry expected of them was the dedication and enthusiasm of the teachers – an integral part of the sheer excellence that was Fezeka under Mr Ngambu's leadership.

Some would call it regimentation. Others would say it was a necessary counterpoise to the harsh environment that slum conditions impose. Whatever it was, it worked. Fezeka was everybody's darling – students thrived, teachers excelled, inspectors (from the Department of Bantu Education) gloated that they had created such perfection.

Despite the fact that the students lived at home, the principal insisted on their conducting themselves as though they were at a boarding-school.

'Do not forget,' he would often urge them, 'you write the same examination as the students at Healdtown, at St Matthew's, at Lovedale.'

Those were among the best schools for Africans in the Cape Province, indeed in the entire country. They were boarding-schools and the experience of the students there was steeped in education and things educational. The experience of students at Fezeka Secondary School approximated that of the boarding-school students as closely as was humanly possible.

Between home and school, mornings and evenings, the student was not allowed to dawdle along the way. As if an enormous gong had sounded, hundreds of students – the boys in grey trousers, white shirts and airforce-blue blazers, and the girls in blazers and pleated skirts of the same colour and white shirts – marched along N.Y. 1, the main road in Guguletu. Students had to join the column at the point of intersection between the side streets where they lived and N.Y. 1. Side streets, by-ways and back streets were off limits to the students.

This movement of students *en masse* fostered punctuality, group identity and high visibility. And this last protected the individual student both from harm by the unruly element that even then stalked the township streets and from falling prey to personal foibles, weaknesses and other counter-productive behaviour. At school, the pace was brisk and businesslike, and emphasised industry.

Aut Primus Aut Cum Primis – Be the First or Among the First! That was the motto of the school. And, daily, the whole school conducted itself in a manner upholding it. At the end of the school day and after a small break, evening studies began.

The students went home only to eat, get themselves ready for the next school day, and to enjoy the barest minimum of sleep. Parents were told, and were glad to hear, that they could forget they had children, in so far as house chores were concerned.

And parents were more than ready to make the sacrifice. They could see for themselves how gainfully employed their children were. Most even said out loud: 'My child is as good as being at a boarding-school.' And that was music indeed to Mr Ngambu's ears.

'Fezeka! Be Perfect!' he reminded the students during assembly whenever he felt they needed reminding. Clearly, this was a man with a dream; even in naming the school that dream had been apparent.

Fezeka. Be Perfect. Fezeka was, comparatively speaking, perfect. Even on Sundays, the students, in full uniform, attended church services at school, just as students did at boarding-schools throughout the country. At this school, I saw School Organisation at work. Marvellously. Right there in the township of Guguletu, with debilitating slum conditions everywhere evident, Mr Ngambu created a healthy, invigorating and challenging centre. He created a place of safety for the students, an oasis, right inside their minds. He gave them direction.

I wouldn't want to mislead anyone, however. It certainly was not tomato sauce all the way. At this school, good as it was, problems of the wider society still touched us. S D was a bright student. In my humble opinion, he had the makings of a great lawyer, an observation that was to become a liability to him. Alarmed that such a talent threatened to go to waste, I took the unusual step of notifying the principal of S D's erratic attendance.

It turned out that Mrs D, S D's mother, had left her employer's telephone number with the principal. You see, S D lived without adult supervision. His mother was a live-in domestic servant. What of the father? Apparently, he had been out of the picture for years. (We were to learn of all this from Mrs D.) Anyway, the mother was summoned to the school.

She had to be made to realise that she was jeopardising the bright future of a singularly gifted student. It was surely our responsibility to help this student towards self-realisation. His mother was clearly a stumbling block in her son's progress. How could she fail to see the obvious? Her son was brilliant. Why did she keep him from school? Clearly, a case of satisfying today's needs with no heed for those of the morrow – so our combined educated minds concluded. We didn't even believe the mother would keep the appointment.

Our fears were laid to rest when, on the appointed day, the young man showed up for school. His mother, he said, would come in the early afternoon, during her afternoon off. The labyrinthine tale that unfolded left me open-mouthed:

S D had told me that his most recent absence, all of two weeks, had been the result of a family bereavement. His sister had died. We were somewhat taken aback, therefore, when Mrs D showed up not wearing black, the colour of mourning. But her exclamation, 'We have not lost a daughter recently', left us eyeing each other uneasily. However, when this lady went on to say, 'We couldn't have. We never had a daughter. He does not have a sister', we turned to the culprit, our eyes like daggers.

Mrs D went on to dismiss all the excuses her son had been dishing out. The principal clearly wanted the boy to himself. He was saying:

'Mrs D, thank you very much for coming. You have certainly clarified the position for us. This young man, rest assured, will get his wages.'

Back in class, I went over S D's story in my mind.

'Ma'm, my sister died,' he had said in a low voice, a voice hoarse with emotion.

'After the funeral mother and some relatives went to a witchdoctor. So for two weeks, the witchdoctor has been working on us and we were told not to come to school.'

Talk about a sucker. I had swallowed it hook, line and sinker (and then some more). But now his back was bare. His lies would no more serve his purpose. When he eventually returned from the principal's office, I confronted him. Understandably, I was upset with him.

'S! How could you lie like this to me?' I snarled, my face, my whole body, every part of it, showing disapproval.

Taking his time, S D uncoiled himself from his seat, strode right up to my table at the front of the classroom. I was standing up. He came and stood right in front of me. Fearlessly, looking me straight in the eye (a tall young man, he had to fold his neck down to do that), he said:

'But Ma'm, do you think my mother would come and admit to you teachers here that she believes in witchcraft?'

And there was a ring of truth to what he was saying.

Our lives are filled with such contradictions. We go to church. We go to the witchdoctor. We go to the doctor. We send our children to school. We believe they can be made to fail their examinations as a result of bewitching by an enemy. We fortify them against such an eventuality with what we believe to be potent medicine from our own witchdoctor or herbalist.

This young man, true to form, our form, the form that was even then shaping him, was conforming. Yes, he was lying. But he did it with such aplomb I could not help admiring him.

His sister had died, he had told me. Even in that lie he'd

been careful not to bring harm to his family. I believe he was deliberate in choosing the subject of his unfortunate fantasy. The 'victim', his sister, was beyond any harm from inadvertent foreshadowing *(ukuhlolela)* on his part. There was no such person!

S D had not 'killed' his mother. He had not 'slain' his brother. Those people were there, susceptible to hurt. In a blink, his lie plunged me back twenty years. I was once more a little girl full of fears, fears that could be brought to the surface at the slightest provocation. Fears that touched on almost all aspects of our daily living. *'Umama wakho uza kuzal' amawele afileyo* – Your mother will give birth to dead twins.' That utterance was enough to send me flying. Such is the power of myth. And S D knew it. He knew that it was deep-rooted in all of us, even educated grown-ups. He understood that we were mealie-meal from the same bag. Oh yes, there is no doubt, we teachers earned our wages.

At Fezeka it was not unusual to find the staffroom reverberating with agitation. Among our favourite topics were politics, education and salaries.

On one such day, we were lamenting the unfairness of the differentiated salary scales for teachers. White teachers earned the highest salaries, followed by coloured and Indian teachers. As in all else that has to do with government bounty, Africans brought up the rear.

With rancour, we held up and demolished the arguments white teachers used to justify their gain. Imitating a white voice:

'I don't know why you people complain. I have a higher standard of living to maintain.

'I'm expected to have a car for myself, a car for my wife and, if my children are of university age, one for each.

'When my children finish high school, they should be able to go to Europe (at least once) where their roots are.

'Do you know how much rent I pay in — [naming a posh white suburb]?'

The windows were rattling. That's how steamed up we were.

'Do they think we went to school all these years, because we aspired to a low standard of living?

'How dare they talk to us about their rent. Is it our choice we live in these hovels?'

We went to town lambasting white teachers – not because the system favoured them, but because they favoured it. They didn't see anything wrong, whereas we saw blatant inequity.

Bank on me to get carried away. Emboldened by the spirit of unity in grief, I forgot myself:

'Do you realise we have the same discrimination right here in this school?' I asked.

'When we passed the matric exams,' I continued, failing to notice the mercury was zooming down with alarming speed, 'my salary went up by five rand a month. You, Stanford, and you, Lucas, got twice that amount by way of increment.'

The words were hardly out of my mouth. The pack barked with discordant voices but one thought.

'No, Sindi! I am a man. I have a wife. I am a breadwinner.'

Pardon me! I had only three children to feed and clothe. And that I was doing solo. But, obviously, to these men, some of whom were yet to marry (never mind have children), I did not qualify as a breadwinner.

When in typical rhinoceros fashion I defended my assertion, attempted to make my African male colleagues see reason, another brother felt I needed further enlightenment and hastened to do his duty to the race:

'What if you were my wife? If we were married and you earned as much as I did you wouldn't respect me.' (That I might actually earn more than he did was beyond this gentleman's powers of imagination.) I was struck by the irony of the situation, reminded of the truth that only the wearer of the shoe can feel the pinch. We were sitting there in that staffroom expecting white teachers to understand our pain, to understand the unfairness of how our salaries were determined. We truly believed that they, with no contact whatsoever with African teachers, ought to see the evil in differentiated salary scales. And here, we Africans, teaching in the same school, in full knowledge of our respective skills, the teaching loads each carried, the level of enthusiasm for work, possession of good work habits, we were not guessing or theorising when it came to ourselves; we knew with intimacy which teacher was capable of what ... and yet, even then, those who were discriminated against failed to see the inherent injustice in the system.

I learned that day that although another may sympathise when I bleed, the tears can only be mine.

Six

Cold stone would have been motivated to action by the atmosphere of studiousness at Fezeka Secondary School. Indeed, many a sluggard was hauled to this school from the only other post-primary school for Africans in the Western Cape, the Langa High School, or from schools in the Ciskei and Transkei. And at Fezeka, whatever had ailed the student – behavioural problems, lack of motivation, uneven or downright poor performance – if it had no organic cause, was soon set right.

In the event, I had come to Fezeka already a little motivated, bringing my big dream of becoming 'Sindiwe Magona – matriculant'. And I was more than half-way there. Four of the required six subjects were in the bag.

At this point in my life, I doubt that I knew any other meaning of the word 'relative' except family. However, working with people, some of whom even had degrees, soon cut my ambition to size.

Nearly all the teachers at this school had matric. Most had a two-year, post-matric teacher's course that was offered at the University of Fort Hare – the SATD (South African Teacher's Diploma). I was one of only three teachers who did not have matric, and all three of us were remedying this deficiency. Which fed the other is hard for me to say. But in the midst of the intellectual activity at Fezeka, I was infected. Apart from the three of us studying for matric, some of the teachers who had SATD were studying for degrees through the University of South Africa, a correspondence university. The students benefited immensely from our immersion in studies.

I had access to the morning newspaper in the staffroom. A few of the teachers lived in the residential areas that were still to be declared 'white', and on their way into the township they bought the morning paper, *The Cape Times*, a newspaper that would only hit the townships towards noon. Township news, news of what happened where we lived, went almost uncovered in the paper. But it was still invaluable as a window to the world out there: in Rondebosch or in Rome, in Plumstead or in Paris, Bellville or Bogota.

I also frequented the public library in those days. My horizon was extending outward in ever-widening circles, although I must confess that the library never became home to me. Knowing you are far from welcome has that effect. I strongly believe that, like reading, frequenting the library is a habit best cultivated very early in life, before starting school. It helped little that I knew that the keepers of the doors were wondering where they had failed, how I had escaped from the mould. To this day I pussyfoot along the stacks whenever I have to go to a library. I doubt I will ever be at ease in those institutions, just as I will never be at ease in restaurants, hotels, theatres, cinemas and all the other places which I never set foot in as a child – where I never saw people like me doing those things that other people who were not black were busy doing with ease and a total lack of self-consciousness. These places are not in my memory, the memory that begins before life begins. The memory of race.

But I was bent on growing, on extending my field of experience, on doing some of those things that for so long had been out of my reach. Now with my glad awakening and the money to indulge my fancies, I bought a radio. Radio Bantu was still based in King William's Town then. I thrilled at news read to me by disembodied voices all those many kilometres away. There were stories. There were songs. There were contests and listeners' queries. Listeners also called in to give birthday greetings to friends or relatives. And I heard and savoured every word. Then disaster opened her eyes and stared me full in the face. Deafness threatened to hinder my progress. Deafness of a special kind. Selective deafness.

Listening to radio programmes, I heard every word – until I ventured into the other languages, English and Afrikaans. Then my problems began. And embarrassment. To say nothing of humiliation.

On a scale of one to ten, I would put my aural ability, then, at five for English and one for Afrikaans. And I so prided myself on my English.

I know from this and later experiences that what I hear depends a lot on my comprehension. My vocabulary and the accent of the speaker help. What blocked my ears then was the absence of a speaker whom I could look at, whose lips I could watch and whose gestures and facial expressions would enhance my ability to decode the message conveyed in these ways.

But, until I tried listening to English programmes on radio, I had not known that I lip-read or that I picked up other cues as well as 'hearing' the words spoken. I am, I believe, a lot more adept these days; practice has made a near-perfect listener of me: in English. The Afrikaans service I abandoned as soon as I got through matric. Of course, for purely selfish reasons, I am sorry today that I did not build on that foundation.

The position at Fezeka improved my situation in more ways than one. Not only did I get the ten rand secondary-school allowance but when after one year at Fezeka I completed matric, I received an additional five rand a month. The more significant change resulting from this job was in my living conditions. For the first time in my life, I had a room to myself: a room of my very own.

As a woman alone, I did not qualify to rent a house in

the township. When my husband was still with me, we had not qualified either. But my position at Fezeka changed all this.

Fezeka Secondary School was run from what had previously been a Catholic hospital. The place abounded with nooks, crannies and little cubicles: no doubt the nuns had used them for bedrooms, chapels and other cells. Those rooms too small to use as classrooms were given to teachers from Fezeka and other schools who, for whichever of the numerous possible official reasons, were without accommodation.

Freed from want, academically upward bound, living on my own, I was ripe for integration into the wider society. My eyes could look a little beyond my nose. I had a roof over my head, food in the pot, clothes to cover my nakedness, a bank account – no matter how little there was in that account. I began to feel the need to set right long-neglected aspects of my life.

Since, with my first pregnancy, I had strayed from the Church, I went to see the Reverend Ndungane about returning. I would have to undergo a process of restoration and attend rehabilitation classes on Saturdays for several months. And so I did.

On Saturday afternoons, at three, a little group of fallen souls congregated at St Mary Magdalene where the rehabilitation classes were held. A lay preacher led the group. We were required to learn by heart Psalm 51. We implored the Almighty to blot out our transgressions, to wash us thoroughly from our iniquity, purge us with hyssop, and have mercy on us. For a whole half a year. Every Saturday we met and confessed our sins and pleaded for forgiveness and restoration to our rightful place as heirs of a loving and compassionate God.

When at last the Church was satisfied that I had repented, that I was cleansed of my iniquity and was now 'whiter than snow', not only would I be welcomed back into the fold but my children would be baptised. More than anything else, this promise of baptism is what prompted me to submit myself to wearing sackcloth and ashes.

Little children die by the score in South Africa. At that time I had no statistics of infant mortality and no knowledge of how African children are overrepresented in this category. But I saw what I saw. Little children's funerals were all too frequent. So I came to believe this was but the nature of things. Children just died more easily, more frequently, than grown-ups.

With three of my own, I feared that sooner or later one or more would die. And how would I bury the unbaptised child whose funeral no priest or lay preacher would lead? I couldn't do that to any child of mine. I would never have forgiven myself if we had had a burial where there was no *mkhokheli*, or leader from the church. My child would have been condemned to eternal damnation, never to go to Heaven.

There must be some law of compensation of which I know nothing, or it was a strange coincidence. Whatever it was, it was a happy coincidence. At the same time that I was publicly denouncing my past errors and terrible sins, I reversed an earlier decision and took a lover. Friends and family, people who had been told 'I'm not interested in men. I'm quite happy on my own', were kind enough to accept what they must have known was inevitable. No one reminded me of my earlier and rather frequent proclamations. I guess I am lucky that way: to be surrounded by an accepting group of people is a source of strength; it frees one to be, to try, to dare. Yes, I am very lucky indeed.

Startling changes were afoot in my family also. Mother agreed about this time to stop deferring a problem that had dogged her since her teens. She became an initiate, the first stage towards becoming a 'witchdoctor', or traditional healer. At the completion of her initiation, my mother would wear an assortment of multi-coloured beads and white traditional clothes, walk barefoot, carry a stick decorated with the tail of her totem animal, *itshoba*, and wear *isidlokolo*, a hat made from the fur of the same or another animal. My mother would also attend witchdoctors' dances. There she would dance the night away to the thuddings of a cow-hide drum or smaller drums made from goatskins. My mother!

Well, Mother's conversion put me in a state of panic. It revealed a side of me even I had hardly suspected. I came out smelling like anything but a rose. I was selfish, egoistic and wholly self-centred. What a raw deal, I thought. Just when I am clawing my way back to respectability. Why is she doing this to me? Was there no end to my humiliation? My mother! And here I was a fully fledged teacher, one with matric, no less. I had been reinstated in the Church. Why was my mother dragging me backwards with her barbaric beliefs? How unlucky can one be? My sorrow, my shame, was keener for the assault on my dignity coming so soon after my restoration to my rightful place. I had not been back long enough in the station of respectability to take it for granted. Like all new converts, I was more zeal than substance.

The confusion, I am happy to say, was brief. Mother wasn't doing anything to me. If she was doing anything to anyone, it was to herself. And in all probability, she was doing something *for* herself. And who was I to judge? Who was I to set standards? What did I know about what she was going through? I am very good at chiding myself. I lashed out now and set my mind straight, unscrambling my knotted brain. Once the truth dawned on me, I was as contrite as I had been condemnatory.

And having thus freed myself, I found I actually enjoyed Mother's new undertaking. When she had a dance, I would tell myself that I would attend until ten or eleven o'clock. But midnight and one o'clock would find me still there. I would be hollering as loudly as the next person. I beat the drums for her and always got carried away and exhausted myself so that the next morning my arms ached.

I learned some of the rituals of the witchdoctors; the way they address one another to show rank among themselves; which ancestors are invoked, in what order, and for what purpose; what the finery they wear signifies; and a host of other things. I came to know and admire the discipline and code of conduct witchdoctors live by. Today, I will say openly to anyone, should it be necessary, 'My mother is a witchdoctor.' I certainly have come a long way from the false sense of shame I used to harbour. I am proud of Mother, for she has travelled very far in her life's journey. And being a witchdoctor is just one more way in which she has amazed me.

Noziganeko is the name of the witchdoctor under whom Mother 'studied'. A large, fierce woman whose knitted brow is her trademark, she is known by the battle name *Nkom'iyahlaba* (Cow that gores). The metaphor alludes to the physical and emotional pain she is capable of inflicting on anyone she finds disrespectful.

A very strict witchdoctor, she would not allow hymns to be used in a dance she attended:

'Let us leave Church things to Church people,' she would say, adding, 'It is good to respect other people's ways even if we do not understand those ways. Only then can we expect them to respect our ways.'

Yes, this lady was proud of her ways and, although she had never set foot inside a classroom, she was learned in the ways of man. 'Live and let live' was her ruling principle. If her eyes fell on the letters of the alphabet, she could not decipher the shapes; yet she had the wisdom of the ages.

Noziganeko also had great respect for school and things of school. Her incredulity, therefore, can be imagined when she found herself a 'consultant' to the teachers of Fezeka Secondary School.

The teachers, when they learned that she had arrived in Cape Town and that her mother tongue remained innocent of English or Afrikaans words, would ask me to ask her for a word.

'Dad'obawo – Father's sister,' I would address her, for she is of the same family as my father, 'one of the teachers at school wants to know the name for the money given as first payment to a witchdoctor before he or she takes on your case.'

'My child,' Aunt Noziganeko would laugh, clapping her hands in disbelief, eyes wide with astonishment, 'teachers don't know that?' When I assured her we really wanted to know, she would tell me the word.

After several such questions and answers, she broke out one day, 'Don't you think I should find myself a teaching job at Fezeka?' In South Africa, people like Aunt Noziganeko are deemed ignorant and what they know of no consequence. Elsewhere on this same globe, they are respected for the knowledge they have. They are valued as resource people. They are paid as consultants. If nothing else, we had demythologised education for her, or at least brought teachers down a little from their pedestals and nearer to ordinary people like her.

Like the dung beetle who cannot see beyond the blade of grass on which she rests, her load totally obscuring her view, I had been overwhelmed first by my fecundity and secondly by finding myself a single parent. My attempts to claw my way out of destitution did little to help me see the wider picture; even when I thought I did, I still fell far short of that goal.

I had no experience of being an adult, having rushed straight from adolescence to middle age. When I was growing up, my individual effort had always met with applause from my parents. When we passed an examination it was customary to be honoured by having something slaughtered in our name. A chicken in lean years and perhaps a sheep in good years.

So it came as quite a shock to me rather late in life to realise that while I was blinded by the brilliance of my goal and the daring of my undertakings, not everyone was impressed. And later, when those labours bore fruit, not all would understand why I was singled out for such good fortune.

At the end of 1969, the close of my first year at Fezeka, I sat for the last two subjects for my matric – Geography and Afrikaans – the former, because I knew no better, and the latter, because it was compulsory.

I was about ten or eleven when I decided I did not want to know any geography. 'What use is this knowledge to me?' I asked myself, no doubt besieged by problems with the subject. 'What does it matter that monsoons bring rain to India and the rice crop can then be planted? Don't I *know* where to get my rice? From the Indian shop at the corner of Fifth Avenue and Main Road.'

At that age, it had appeared right, not to mention convenient, that I stop cracking my poor skull learning of rainfall and industries in lands far, far away. I was convinced I would never see those lands. Nothing in my immediate experience had encouraged me to think I might even see another part of South Africa.

Geography had the distinction of increasing my knowledge of the matric grading system. I achieved a grade that prompted me to investigate its meaning.

'What does the symbol *Fx* mean?' I asked someone at the Circuit Office in town. 'It is a condoned pass,' I was informed.

I grasped at the noun. Pass. I had passed a subject I knew absolutely nothing about. I was beside myself. The requirements of the examination body satisfied, I awaited my matric certificate, although by now I also had an inkling that matric did not amount to much. Still, I was happy at what I had achieved. Sindiwe Magona – matriculant!

Working full-time, mothering solo, I had completed a

two-year course – in two years. What is more, I had managed to convince myself that I had a brain, a working brain, although I had left school six years before and despite the fact that I had children.

No greater sin can a woman commit than having children. That is the lesson I was learning. 'She has children' quickly quenched any fiery ardour, put paid to protestations of undying love; no fool would dream of marrying a woman who had children. It was common practice for women to hide the fact of their motherhood. They were stamped as damaged goods in the pure minds of men whose reputations remained untarnished despite their fathering offspring. Indeed, rather than detracting from it, a man's stature grew in direct proportion to the number of women he had impregnated.

The censure came from women as well as from men. Their agreement about the correct behaviour for women with children chilled me to the marrow. Married, divorced, widowed and single mothers were lumped together. Mothers, it was clear in the minds of the vast majority, had no business being anything else. But I had dreams yet.

My alarm grew with the discovery that I was expected, calmly and mother-like, to await old age and death. My sole and consuming interest had to be the children. I was only twenty-five and wanted to believe more awaited me in life.

As I carried books with the surreptitiousness of a kleptomaniac, derision followed me from real, no-nonsense mothers who, highly satisfied with being mothers and nothing but mothers, found my behaviour rather weird if not wanton.

'What! What are those things you're carrying? They look like books.'

We are standing in a long queue, waiting for a bus that is taking its own sweet time. To ward off boredom, eyes rove in search of escape, of interesting topics. Obviously, I qualify. The question triggers a panic reaction in me as all eyes, accusing, suspicious, disbelieving, querying, turn my way.

'Yes, they are books,' I hear myself croak. I am apologetic, pleading for the topic to be dropped. Judges, however, know no mercy.

'Why are you carrying books? Don't you have children?'

I reply that yes, I do have children. Somehow I feel as though I am confessing to a felony: guilty as charged. And by the time I finish my lame explanation of the contraband, all idle chatter has stopped. Eyes stare. Twitters threaten. And then some brave soul breaks the silence.

Clapping hands in utter consternation, the woman I do not know belts out in time to the claps, *'Yho! Yho! Yho!'*; *clap-clap-clap* go her hands, in perfect unison. Then, with still enough breath left to utter a complete sentence, she continues:

'Whuwow! Ngathi ndiyazibona ndipheth'iincwadi! Ndakugqib'ukuba nabantwana! Yhu!' (Wow! I can just see myself carrying books. After I have children! Gee!)

I wish I could say I braved such scorn because the opinion of others mattered little to me. That I was a trendsetter and not one to swim with the tide. But I would be lying. I was a frightened little person who thought everyone else but me had a survival kit up her sleeve.

Gradually, I started branching out and growing, despite my need for other people's approval. Through work, through church and through my studies, I met new friends. One of these prevailed upon me to join the National Council of African Women. Until early in 1969 I hardly knew of the organisation. And it is the oldest in the history of our organisations, renowned as they are for the brevity of their lives. This organisation opened my eyes to prevailing social ills. Not to anything I had not seen or known existed, but now for the first time, through discussion and action by members, I began to see myself as someone who could do something out there – away from family, job, neighbour or friend.

Lending a hand was not a concept foreign to me. No.

What was was that the hand could be mine, that I had the right and, indeed, the obligation to intervene in situations of distress. Other people's distress.

Perhaps it had not occurred to me that I had anything to offer. In this respect, the National Council of African Women taught me I was grown up. I could assume social responsibility. People's burdens could be eased, if only I lifted a finger.

And having woken up to my social duty, I inflicted it on everyone who could not escape my new-found, zestful enthusiasm.

Seven

Fortune smiled my way, and in 1970 I left Bantu Education for Bantu Administration, nearly doubling my monthly earnings from forty-seven to seventy-two rand. But for every blessing there is a sacrifice.

If Mr Tabane, the principal of Moshesh Higher Primary School, had been chagrined when I left that school, the principal of the school I was leaving now, Fezeka Secondary, was irate.

'Mistress, now that I have scrubbed you, they all want you.' With those words, Mr Tabane had expressed regret at my leaving, conveniently forgetting he had not exactly welcomed me with open arms on my arrival at Moshesh. But we parted with smiles, handshakes, and a little teasing: 'They have no netball team to talk about, Mistress. We'll outdistance you as horses outrun donkeys.'

Mr Ngambu, upon learning of my intentions, simply turned to ice. And the next day he told me:

'We are going to need the room, Mistress.'

'The room' was large: a bedroom with a dining-room, living-room, kitchen, bathroom and foyer. It had inside running water, hot as well as cold. It had electricity. Unusual for an African township? You bet! Was Mr Ngambu justified in throwing me out? As a woman, I had absolutely no hope of being allowed to rent or buy a council house.

A great injustice was being done to me. This was my feeling, one that underscored the enormous power people in high positions wield. Granted, I conceded, he must be upset that I am leaving the school, particularly at this time of year:

July, right after the beginning of the second half of the school year. But it was not as if he would be stranded without a teacher for long. Then, as now, there were always teachers looking for positions. But not only were there teachers who did not teach at Fezeka living on the premises, there were unoccupied rooms. And there were people living there who were not teachers at all.

'Why is he being so vindictive?' my new boss, Mr Victor Taylor, queried upon learning of my eviction. I learnt a new English word. Vindictive. Hitting back. *Ukuziphindezela* is what I knew was taking place.

Bantu Administration is the branch of government charged specifically with the regulation of Africans. In the urban areas of South Africa at that time this function was performed by local authorities: in the Western Cape, the Cape Divisional Council and the Cape Town City Council. I worked for the latter, the CCC, and learned a lot about my special hell as an African.

The first thing I learnt was that I was allowed to help only people from Langa and Guguletu. Nyanga, administered by the Cape Divisional Council, did not come under the agency where I worked. These three townships and some smaller locations in the farming areas were the only areas where Africans could live, legally, in the Western Cape, according to the Group Areas Act.

Although I worked in the Welfare Section of this organisation, I was near enough to the pass office, which was the control tower, to get to know its practices and to witness the translation of vile laws, their blind application and the horrendous outcomes they had.

Ninety-nine per cent of the cases we handled were, in one way or another, spawned by such laws.

The pass office housed rows and rows of files, walls of files, in numerous rooms. These were personal files, the records kept of all Africans who had been in the 'designated' area for any significant length of time. Names, dates, places of birth, sex, tribe, mother tongue, names of parents, places of origin and more were recorded in these files. This information was reflected on a person's reference book or pass.

The pass was a document which Africans were until fairly recently forced to carry from age sixteen and which they had to produce whenever a policeman requested it. It told the authorities why that African was in that particular urban area at that time. In my first pass, the reason for my presence in the Cape Town area was given as:

'For purposes of residing at N.Y. 12 No. 6, Guguletu.' This was my home address. I was, at that time, a student teacher.

Later, my pass would have these endorsements:

'For the purpose of: Working for the Nyanga School Board.' That was in 1962.

Though I did not work long for the School Board in Nyanga my pass failed to reflect this, for the simple reason that I did not notify the authorities as required. That is, until it became absolutely necessary that I do so. The next endorsement:

'Working for Mrs— of [giving an address]' is a sample.

This last endorsement was repeated several times as I changed 'medems' the way madams change stockings: frequently.

'Working for the Langa School Board.'

This one, of course, came with the Moshesh Higher Primary School post.

'Working for the Cape Town City Council.'

I had arrived, I believed. The CCC jobs were very prestigious in the townships. And in Langa the Welfare Section was seen as the cat's pyjamas. Mr Taylor, the Supervisor, had a very good reputation not only among his staff but also among the African staff at the Administration Office, so this endorsement represented quite a leap in my image of myself as a worker.

The files at the pass office were active files, those of

Africans living in the area, working Africans, Africans on old age pension or disability grant, or students. The files of those who had died and those who had been away for very long periods and were presumed dead or living illegally elsewhere were in the archives.

Then there was the category none of the white staff ever said anything about to black staff – the files in the strong-room, under lock and key: files with damaging information about dangerous people. Dangerous to the state, that is.

Though liberal in the South African context, the City Council could not ameliorate the harsher laws, rules and regulations governing Africans. It did, however, turn a blind eye here, bend a rule there and deliberately misinterpret a regulation elsewhere. And, as we were to see later when Bantu Administration Boards took over from the City Council the task of regulating the lives of Africans, the Council was not as vigorous in pursuing government policy as the government would have liked it to be. However, even with such benevolent influence, I had not been in Bantu Administration long before I found its machinations staggering in scope, evil in execution and crushing in effect.

Under normal circumstances, a child would not have anything to do with the pass office until age sixteen. At that time, the young person would have to go and get a pass or reference book, also called a *dompas* (stupid pass). Children were registered at birth so that their names would appear in the files of their parents. At sixteen, therefore, African youngsters duly presented themselves armed with birth certificates, proving that they were was born in the prescribed area, and records of school attendance, proving continuous residence within the area.

Forms were then completed, and fingerprints, thumb-prints and palmprints taken and sent to Pretoria.

Weeks or months later, the reference book arrived. Notification of this was sent and the applicant fetched it from the Department of Bantu Administration, a more august body

housed in Standard House in the white suburb of Observatory.

The little black book was the most important document
in South Africa for an African. A more hated document was
hard to find. People sold their very souls to obtain one
endorsed for an urban area where they wanted to work and
where, according to the law, they had no right to be.

Like an umbilical cord, the pass office was the direct link
between the government and the African. And the one-way
force-feed was bitter and poisonous.

The pass office was not used by Africans only. Often, to
hurry things up, white employers accompanied their workers there when they came for registration.

One day, a horse-racing tycoon felt like seeing for himself
where his 'boys' lived. The boys ranged in age from fifteen
to fifty and more. They had had to pass a selection test to
get the job: look brawnier than the rest of the herd from
which they were handpicked, more alert, more eager to do
the master's bidding. Now under contract to work for him
for eleven months of the year, they were housed in what
were euphemistically referred to as 'single men's hostels'.
These places were not hostels nor did they house single
men (or men only, for that matter). Most of the migrant
workers, very much married, left wives and children behind
in the reserves.

The colleague who had taken the horse-racing tycoon to
view the barracks later told us that on seeing one of them,
this gentleman had remarked:

'I wouldn't let my horses live in this.'

The Welfare Section where I worked dealt with anyone who
cared to seek counsel there. Cases ranged from assistance
with applications for old age pensions, disability grants,
scholarships and bursaries, rent remissions, unpaid wages,
workman's compensation and problems with breaches of
contract, to domestic disputes, child support and housing.

Mostly, though, our job consisted in deciphering for our bewildered clients that particular law, rule or regulation that was the cause of their problems.

Just when I thought I had become immune to the inhumanity of what went on at the pass office, I was overwhelmed by an episode involving a family of fifteen who were being evicted from the house they had rented for years.

It had suddenly come to the attention of the authorities that a two-roomed house was grossly over-occupied, even by the far-from-healthy practices of the township.

What had once been the home of a couple was now occupied by the widow (a grandmother by now) and her three daughters, who had between them eleven children. Yes, fifteen people somehow managed to cram themselves into an area that could not have been more than ten square metres.

The authorities were greatly stirred.

'Clearly,' announced the alarmed office, 'this situation is not tenable! It is unhealthy.'

Whilst I and, I'm sure, many another rational people would agree with the diagnosis, the proposed remedy stunned all who came to hear of it. It devastated the family in question.

'Out! Now! Out!' ordered those in power, unmoved by the beseeching tenants.

Upon representation by one of my colleagues, the officer handling this case explained as if to a retarded six-year-old:

'Mrs Mtetwa, what would the world think of us if they heard we put fifteen people into such a tiny space?'

It had escaped this gentleman's realisation that cleaning up the country's image abroad was a severe handicap to this family, who were not being offered alternative accommodation.

It took a lot of negotiation, including roping in influential whites, for the authorities to see their way clear to allowing this family to remain in their home.

And then, insidiously, what I had found shocking when I had first come to do this work began to shock me less and less. But then one cannot make an inventory at each day's end of one's emotional reactions to the absurd, the grotesque and even the criminal.

Had this blunting of my emotions stopped at that failure to notice, to feel and to register shock, it might have been tolerable. What shook me to the very core of my being was when I found myself thinking in this fashion:

A family presented itself at my office seeking help in reinstating an eighteen-year-old son. The young person had broken the requirement of continuous residence in the Western Cape and therefore could no longer legally live with his parents. He had gone to live with one of his grandmothers when he was ten years old. This lady had now passed away. Naturally, he and his parents assumed his place was with his parents.

They had already been to the pass office and been turned away. I was their last hope and I found myself thinking: 'But how *can* they expect to get permission for him to live in Cape Town? After all, he *has* been away for eight years.'

I was in the professional process of explaining the whys and wherefores of the case to this family, busy being the excellent tool the government needed in enforcing its 'law', actually 'helping' the clients comprehend their situation so that they could then make rational decisions, decisions not in conflict with government policy, when the eighteen-year-old challenged me:

'But, Ma'am, what would have happened had I been a white child?' ... thus thawing my frozen soul, loosening my calcified brain.

With our extended family system, grandparents, aunts, uncles and other relatives have access to our children – as help in the home, as company and to enable us to cope better by having fewer children actually living with us. Or for no reason at all except that the child would like to go and live with them or they would like to have the child living with them.

Such arrangements are an integral aspect of our wholeness. We are a family-oriented people and our families are gloriously more inclusive than those of white South Africa.

As a child I had often wondered how the men who emptied the lavatory buckets could do such a job. Along the highway on the outskirts of Langa grow trees that are all bent in the same direction: trained by the south-easterly winds. The shape of these trees is something else I have long found intriguing. Misshapen and twisted souls.

Then, unbidden, the answer came to me.

On an official round one day visiting homes, I came across this scene:

Right there on the street, a pot of mealie-meal porridge boils. The primus stove on which it perches precariously looks absurd – flimsy flame barely discernible, so much outdone by the sun's cruel brilliance.

Willy-nilly all round, on street, on pavement, on scraggly patch of grass beyond the road, furniture, suitcases, bundles of clothing, pots, pans and other sundries lie strewn. Standing guard over this wealth, belongings now testifying to life gone askew, are three young people: probably the 'children'.

Eviction! Did Not Pay Rent! One glance was all I needed.

The beautiful wardrobes, mirrors shimmering in the bright noon-day sun, provoked anger in me. These people only had themselves to blame, I fumed silently. Who asked them to saddle themselves with debt? Look at those wardrobes. Small wonder they couldn't afford the rent. No sense of priorities, I bristled.

Psychologists call my kind of response habituation.

Habituation: familiarity that comes with frequent exposure or repetition; becoming accustomed to what was once staggering, bewildering or upsetting. The gnarled trees along the highway, the *kakabhali* (shit bailiff) of my childhood, and I well trained to accept the intolerable.

It is generally known that in South Africa the laws have broken up families, African families. I can vouch for that. I know one family, at least, that the government tore apart as sure as if it had physically pulled husband and wife asunder.

Was it shame? Was it lack of trust? When he left me, was he planning to get back to Cape Town under contract, and not let on to me? Did he encounter difficulties in getting a contract? Did he give up? Was it pride? Sadly, I will never know the answer to these and many more questions about my life.

Curiosity overcame me one day, and I went and looked into my husband's file.

In 1966 my husband, I found, had been endorsed out of the area. I discovered that he had been a 10(l)(d) – a migrant labourer with an annual contract who had to go home each year. I was a 10(l)(b) – one who had legal rights to live in Cape Town. I held that file for the longest minute I have ever known while thoughts raced through me. Then I put it back. And walked away. We never really had a chance, I realised. We were fools to have married. We had not had an inkling about what we were pitting ourselves against. Gross lack of awareness had made us naturals for our break-up. Indeed, we had not even known we were pitting ourselves against anything. Definitely not against the state, the mighty government. Against all that power, just the two of us. No wonder we were pulverised.

Had we been older or wiser, we would have thought a hundred thousand times before embarking on a venture so fraught with difficulties and insurmountable obstacles. At least, I would have.

Oh, yes! It was instructive working here. A microcosm of the wider society. The hierarchy was white-topped and black heavy. White people in South Africa regard themselves as superior. The social environment reinforces that. The law upholds it. Racism is accepted. It is the traditional way of life, perfectly normal.

The whites who worked in the Bantu Administration offices had a lot going for them. They received inflated salaries, even by white South African standards.

Included in their pay cheque was an additional amount: compensation. That was for the daily insult to their dignity of working with Africans. Another hidden benefit to them was the absence of competition. Once in, they were in for life.

As a group, whites enjoyed preference in the labour market as in everything else. They were assured of always being in positions of authority. Therefore, not too many sought these positions at the Bantu Administration offices. Most could find jobs elsewhere. Obviously most, if not all, of those whites who ended up 'serving' Africans couldn't make it in the white world. But those Africans who made it to these same 'office' jobs were, by and large, the cream of the crop. They had nowhere else to go.

Often, the result was that well-educated blacks remained in positions of perpetual subordination to the not-so-well-educated whites. The African staff knew this, but we were also extremely grateful for the 'beige collar' jobs. Many a high-school graduate was in domestic work, in the mines and elsewhere doing menial work.

That is not to say, however, there was no resentment. The Africans were sore that they should be paid less than their supervisors, whose jobs, more often than not, they'd had to teach them. The whites, on the other hand, were none too thrilled about 'colleagues' they could never accept as such.

The white clerk, daily reminded that he had ended up working 'for' and with the wretched of his land, daily affirmed his superiority. His 'colleagues' bore the brunt of his strivings for psychological release.

Word got out that most of these 'monsters' who screamed obscenities at people they perceived as less human than themselves were actually 'normal people' in another world. From time to time one of us would bump into one of them over weekends. And he would be doing something normal people do. And doing it in a normal way.

What metamorphosis had to take place each evening, we wondered.

In 1973, the government decided its policies for regulating Africans were not succeeding. Blame for the failure was put at the doorstep of local authorities:

'If we want our policies to succeed,' said one government spokesman, 'we must put at the helm people who believe in them!'

Bantu Administration changed hands. Bantu Administration Boards were created, replacing the functions formerly carried out by city and divisional councils. Now the African would come directly under the heavy hand of the Afrikaner, the government, with no mitigating influence whatsoever. This was the last straw, the final push I needed to leave. For some time I had been unhappy with what I was doing. But I had not had the strength to throw away what seemed a good job, a job whose equivalent I was highly unlikely to find elsewhere. That kind of recklessness needs practice. It needs examples. And I was still trying to get good jobs. What, then, would I know of throwing them away? This was my conflict until the decision was taken out of my hands with the advent of the Bantu Administration Boards.

It was not long after this that I resigned. I gave up my post of welfare worker and shed any illusion that there existed for the profession of social work a way of serving the African population in South Africa. Government legislation and government policy, relentless in its efforts to destroy the African people, would not promote social services that might benefit Africans. For that would be counter-productive.

During the first month when the Bantu Administration Boards took over from the local authorities, I was serving notice of termination of service. I feared becoming blunted to the pain I was witnessing daily, the pain that daily assaulted my consciousness. In vain attempt at professional distancing I would display a cool exterior whilst I burned inside with the blood from my pierced heart.

Often I found myself forced to excuse myself in the middle of an interview, overwhelmed by the client's pain, overwhelmed by the hopeless service I could render.

I quit social work. I had come to understand that it could not be practised at that place, at that time, under the prevailing social conditions.

Eight

Sandile was becoming adventurous.

'Stop, Sandile!'

'Stop' stopped, stuck in my throat. I feared feminising him. And that seemed highly probable to me since he had no father to counterbalance my influence.

Daily, therefore, I was tested bitterly as I swallowed my wise injunctions: 'Don't, Sandile' remained unsaid as my son, proud as a warrior returning victorious from battle, narrated his adventures of that day:

'*Sisi*, I went to the swimming pool all by myself today!'

He had to cross N.Y. 1, the busiest street in Guguletu, to get there. I die while pasting a smile on my face.

'Gee! You are certainly becoming big, aren't you?' And to put in a safety valve of sorts I add, 'Do you remember how we cross a busy road? A road with many cars?'

Yes, he assures me, he knows. 'You look this way and that way and that way and you cross.'

Perhaps a frown or another cue comes out from within me when the minister is visiting and you, proud parent, want to impress him with the discipline of your home. Or could it be that the forced smile on my face is not as reassuring as I think? Whatever it is, he realises or remembers and adds, 'Quickly!'

I smile and pat him on the head. 'Dear God,' I think to myself, 'he's forgotten the most important part. The one before quickly.'

Later in the afternoon, I will go over the rules for crossing the road: Look this way – and that way. Look *this* way, again. IF YOU DO NOT SEE A CAR – cross, quickly.

In raising my voice, almost screaming as I say the crucial phrase, I hope it sinks into his brain. 'Please God,' I pray.

But the next day I have to leave him to his devices as I go to work. I console myself that even had I been home, he would be roaming the streets of Guguletu, for that is the nature of Guguletu childhood. My fears are not quelled by the knowledge.

The problem of children, their safety and welfare was becoming burdensome. In so far as my own life kept branching out, the less adequate I felt as a mother. And neither had I started out likely to win any prizes in motherhood.

It is a never-ending source of mystification to my mother that God saw fit to give me not one but three children.

'Hayi wena Sindi, mntan'am, uthixo wafana nje wakunik' abantwana, bade babathathu. Awunabubele tu. – No. You, Sindi, my child, God just gave you not one but three children. You are totally without motherly kindness.'

My children agree with Mother's assertion. Not in so many words, no. But even as toddlers they showed a marked preference for her house to mine. As they grew older there were occasions when I had physically to haul them back to our home, reminding them that that was what it was. Our home: theirs and mine.

In all seriousness, though, upon completing matric, I didn't quite know how to proceed. It is not as if even I thought I could just up and go, leaving three children with Mother. Years earlier, she had been quite prepared to take Thembeka and four-month-old Thokozile when I had wanted to go to Durban's King Edward VIII Hospital to train as a nurse.

But there is a big difference between two children and three children. Moreover, my husband had forbidden me to go and, although he left me a year later, we were still married. He had legal authority over me. I did not trust him not to foul things up for me if I pursued that route, even though he had left me.

I did not even raise the nursing option with Mother again. We had both been devastated when, with all arrangements in place, my husband had stopped me from taking the first step to becoming a nurse. Since it happened in 1965 we have never spoken of that terrible blow.

However, above all these problems there loomed another: Father took ill. For more than a year, except for uncharacteristic tiredness and infrequent pain, his condition did not appear to get worse. However, since I had never seen Father ill, that he now was poorly was sufficient cause for worry.

Besides Father's illness, besides the studies in which I immersed myself, and besides job and social responsibilities, there was another reason for my deficiency or lack of enthusiasm for motherhood.

The second of eight children, I was mothering by age seven. I took care of Mawethu, six years younger than me and next in line (of the seven surviving children). I washed his nappies to a sparkling, spot-free whiteness despite the absence of detergent. I cooked his meals. And in those days baby food still lumped when you mixed the powdered milk with boiling water. And glass still cracked and broke if you poured liquid half a degree above lukewarm into it. Many are the thrashings I received because in the middle of the night I had broken the baby's only bottle. I also kept Mother's hands free for her other chores by keeping Mawethu on my back. I mothered him every day after school. And all day long on Saturdays: Mother has been an inveterate horserace-goer for decades. Of the four children after him, I helped raise three. Thembani, the baby, is the only one I didn't look after. I was away at College when he was born.

By the time I had my first baby, therefore, I was an old hand in the mothering business. So I didn't go all ga-ga over my own babies. Who would, after raising five? That is not to say I was ready to put them in jeopardy.

More and more, living with me began to look hazardous. I couldn't get their laundry done. I wasn't there most mealtimes on most days. And the menace of the car was growing in the townships – narrow streets, old cars in dire need of repair, and unlicensed and often drunk drivers contributed generously to that development.

Thembeka, older, more capable of doing things for herself, posed the least problem. But the younger children highlighted my inadequacy as a mother and the question of their safety.

While I toiled by day, studied by night and attended this or that meeting in between, Sandile prowled the streets in search of adventure. He soon wearied of the Community Centre opposite Mother's; not enough excitement, I suppose. The L-shaped row of tiny shops behind the Civic Hall held special fascination, as did the swimming pool, the milkman's push-cart, the fisherman's horse-drawn cart, and the cars of the University of Cape Town students who were doing research at the Community Centre.

To establish rapport with their subjects, the white students gave the children rides in their cars. At sight of these cars, the children would swarm like bees to flowers, with cries of 'David! David!' or 'Suzeen! Suzeen!' or some other name thrown out with uncharacteristic familiarity that would wane as years advanced, sweeping away both childlike charm and the benign unawareness of rank which is so much a mark of youth.

These cries of utter joy would pour out of the houses, from street corners, from back yards, from wherever the fans happened to be when the students came bringing this rare treat. Close behind the cries, stubby legs would come propelling their owners towards these new-found friends.

I knew that one day there would be an accident. One of these giddy students would kill one of these silly children who knew nothing of the dangers of cars. I also knew that child would be my Sandile.

One bleak afternoon in May, my worries about Sandile climaxed. I was still working in Langa then. Mr Siboma, a colleague, came into the office, having been out on business. His black-as-night skin had turned ashen, so shaken he was.

There had been an accident in Guguletu, he told us. A horrible accident.

'A little boy's been run over by a bus. Killed on the spot.'

Mr Siboma then told us the accident had taken place at N.Y. 1, near Kirk's, the Section Two Administration Office. 'How old was he, Siboma? How old?' I could hear my voice, octaves too high. My body, on the other hand, was numb. Only my heart lived. Doing somersaults.

Siboma stretched out his right arm in front of him and, palm facing down, said, 'This high.'

That was the exact height of Sandile. But I saw myself square my shoulders, brace my chin, and cling to any straw I could lay my hands on.

'What was he wearing? What was he wearing, Siboma?' Surely, it could not be my child.

I don't remember whether the answer was red shorts and blue shirt or green shorts and blue shirt. But whatever it was, a picture of Sandile clad in those exact clothes jumped into my mind's eye.

In an instant I knew, the way only a mother can know when her child's life is in peril. He was lying, plastered like a tube of toothpaste split open and flattened onto the uncaring road.

Mr Siboma had returned at about three o'clock. We knocked off at five. Those two hours were the longest, most torturous hours of my life.

Without a word I left the little gathering that had formed itself around Siboma. My feet grew eyes and led me to my office where I dropped into a chair and fearfully waited for the phone to ring.

Half an hour after I'd known my son was dead, the phone remained stubbornly silent. I understood. Of course, it was too soon. Mother was still in shock. The ambulance had not yet arrived. A doctor had to say the 'He is dead'. They were still hoping against hope, waiting for the doctor's verdict. That would wipe away the last vestige of hope.

An hour passed. Any minute now, the phone telling me to come home. Of course, not wanting to alarm me, the caller would not give me the reason. Only the summons.

But I would know. I knew now.

'Come home,' I would hear.

An hour and a half had come and gone. Of course! How stupid of me. Knowing we were brought home by van, they would wait for the van to bring me home at five. Meanwhile, I could see the human traffic at Mother's.

Sweaty figures grunting, bent over furniture. Lifting. Carrying out of the house. Rooms cleared, bare of their familiar holdings. The wake would start that very evening.

Some people tried to con me into believing I was mistaken, might be mistaken. I refused to allow hope into my bleeding heart. Others, more level-headed, advised me to defer mourning until the sad news was imparted to me officially and in the customary manner.

They could afford to be philosophic. It was not their child's bones that had been crushed to pulp by the thick, black heartless tyres of a double-decker bus.

Until that afternoon, I had never counted the stops the van made before it came to N.Y. 74, my street; all the way almost to the other side, the outskirts of the township. In fact, I was the last stop.

The usual thirty minutes' drive felt like thirty long hours or more. When we drew near the scene of the accident, I asked Mr Siboma to let me off the van. Usually accommodating, today he hid behind City Council rules: he wasn't allowed to make unscheduled stops, he reminded me sheepishly.

Finally, the van left N.Y. 1 and turned left into N.Y. 50. Then, a second or two later, it turned right into N.Y. 68 and immediately turned left into my side of the crescent-shaped street where I lived.

Thirty yards ahead I expected to see, higgledy-piggledy, the innards of our house laid out in the sun. No, the yard wore its customary clutter, no more.

Knowing my mother, I was not at all surprised by the bare yard. Neither did it fool me. I could almost hear her forbidding people from clearing the house before I arrived.

'Do you want my child to die in the van? Can't you see that the shock of a death when there was no illness as she left this morning will kill her?'

'S-thsi, Sthsi, Stshisthsi! Nank'uSthisthi!' (Sisi, Sisi. Here is Sisi!) Sandile had a lisp at that age. There he was, standing at the door, a grin the shape of a watermelon slice on his face as the van drew to a patient stop in front of my mother's house: N.Y. 74 No. 33.

I burst into tears.

You can say I worried about my son. And I worried about worrying so about him. Would he grow up dove-hearted? Was I overprotective? Would he be a sissy, ridiculed mercilessly by men and shunned by women, scorned by the old, and ragged by the young?

So intense was my determination to raise my children the way I had been raised, the only way I knew how – with discipline, providing for their needs – that I hurled myself into the rebuilding of what I thought of as 'financial security'. Yes, the man who fathered them had left. I, their biological mother, had remained with them. However, I can assure you, my children never had a mother. I was too busy being their father. I worked at more than one job at any given time. I studied by correspondence, which was supplemented with tutorials.

I told them: 'You are not going to run wild. People

expect you to because you are being raised with no father. Well, what would a father do for you that I do not do? I pay rent, buy food, clothes and school uniforms; I pay school fees and doctor's fees when you're not well.' The list was long, the drilling hard. Corporal punishment galore.

My worst fears were always just under the skin, ready to pop out full-blown at the slightest suggestion of a problem. If one of the children took a toy from another child I saw a highway to jail. I knew the boy, Sandile, would be kicking all of us, the two girls and myself, by the time he was nine years old. He would bully us, three frail women too weak to fight him effectively. And the girls? By age twelve, if I were not hard on them, I just knew they would be mothers, pre-teen mothers, and that would be the end of whatever future they might have.

Were my fears unfounded? Gloomy and pessimistic?

Perhaps. But these things were happening right in front of my eyes. And most of the young people who did them even had fathers.

In this respect, the South African Committee for Higher Education (SACHED) where I attended tutorials was invaluable, offering not only an opportunity to study but a support group, people who could give me some perspective on children, education, the economy, politics, and other issues in a seemingly effortless manner.

I had become a student at SACHED when, after I had completed matric, my incurable optimism propelled me to tackle the General Certificate of Education. I enrolled with the University of London, doing the GCE by correspondence as I had done matric. I had hopes of one day landing a scholarship to England.

At SACHED, I was to meet a small group of young people who, like me, went on believing in themselves and in the possibility of a better tomorrow despite all the pointers to the contrary.

SACHED had itself grown out of the need to redress the

injustice of a segregated higher education that effectively barred access to all students who had not been born with a pink skin. By providing books, tuition-fee advances, tutors, rooms with electric lights, tables on which to work, a kitchen and a bathroom complete with a bath, SACHED answered the physical and basic needs of students – needs that effectively crippled and stunted thousands upon thousands of students (and their families) simply because they were black.

SACHED also helped black students overcome some of the obstacles in their way: city and municipal libraries were not open to Africans, for example. SACHED arranged that we obtain permission to use the libraries since we were doing university work. We had the same arrangement with the University of Cape Town about the use of its library. Tutors, mainly from this same university, came and helped us with our course work, at five rand an hour. In the event, many did not even claim the payment but tutored us out of their generosity.

Besides material support, SACHED also provided a place where encounters of a rare kind took place. It was there that I began to be what I had been barred since birth from becoming: truly South African. SACHED afforded me the opportunity to meet, interact with and get to know people who were classified differently from me. I met a spectrum of South Africans. Different shades of black, different mother tongues, different economic and educational backgrounds, those whose ancestors had come from India and those whose ancestors had come from Europe: people whose ancestors and cultures were poles apart. Suddenly, I was part of a brilliant rainbow, partaking of the wealth of human diversity that is South Africa's.

I was preparing for the GCE exams when Father died. He passed away on a Thursday. Five days before, I had seen him at Groote Schuur Hospital where he was a patient. It was an afternoon so clear that, walking up from the Main Road to the hospital, one could almost see the leaves of the trees gracing the slopes of Devil's Peak.

During the visit Father said what were to be his very last words to me:

'You have been blessed, my daughter. You are very wealthy.' Then he stopped and I thought he had finished. But no, he went on: 'Look at your friends. There is everybody in your group of friends.'

I understood. The little group of SACHED students, my friends, standing around his bed could have posed for a photograph entitled: The Peoples of South Africa. Abubakar Solomons, Rachmat Omar, Farieda Khan and Zubeida Desai were with me that day. There, beside the deathbed of a man classified 'Bantu', were people not of that classification, people who were not Father's employers or supervisors but friends: his daughter's and therefore his.

When visiting-time was up, we left. And I bade my father goodbye. An ordinary goodbye. Why hadn't I somehow felt this was the last, the very last time I would see him alive, breathing, talking, his eyes with their fire?

Five days later he was no more. The hospital notified the police to notify us. The police bungled. They went and told strangers, who couldn't have cared less about Father or that he had died. Instead of N.Y. 74 No. 33 the police went to N.Y. 94 No. 33 where nobody knew the man whose death they came to report. This was just one more result of our having been uprooted from our stable residential areas. In Blouvlei, Retreat, everyone would have known Tolo. They would have recognised the surname Magona. And, what is more, had the police by some strange coincidence happened on people who were new in the area, those people would have taken the trouble of asking their next-door neighbours if they knew such a name. Blouvlei was that kind of a place; the people there real people, good people.

When the family at N.Y. 94 said they knew no one of that

name, the police did what they do best – put it down to the unfathomable stupidity of 'those township kaffirs' – blaming the victim. The hospital could not notify us of Father's death because we didn't have a phone. And because of the indifferent transport system, Father had eventually stopped Mother from visiting him in the evenings. 'Please tell your mother to stop coming here at night,' he had asked me, adding, 'After she has gone, I can't sleep, worrying about her, about when she'll get home and whether she will be safe.' And I, dutiful daughter, had prevailed on Mother only to go and see her husband of thirty-three years during the weekend. But to the police, it was our fault. If we didn't care enough about Father, why should they take the extra step of ascertaining that the family of this man was notified of his passing away?

The police had access to at least two voluminous files on Father, at the Department of Bantu Administration in Observatory. Files with all sorts of details about Father. But they couldn't find his family to tell them of his death. Fixed by the pass laws to the same residential area, we had been living at the same address for years. But the police couldn't locate us.

So we didn't hear of Father's death at Groote Schuur Hospital until three days later.

The following week, when the coloured man from the Cancer Society brought the last food parcel, we knew he knew. His tear-filled eyes as he handed us the box told us he knew. We would not see him again. I didn't even know his name. But he cried when father died.

Nine

Whatever intellectual or political awakenings have occurred in my life began at SACHED.

Blindly following in my idol's footsteps, I had applied to SACHED. Was that not how my beloved brother, Jongilizwe, had studied for the British university entrance examinations? Armed with the General Certificate of Education, he had left South Africa for Oxford in 1965.

Lindy Wilson was running SACHED when I became a student there. And although I'm sure I did not think so at the time, Lindy is a survivor.

Many would not think of white South Africans as people with anything to survive. I know that the concept is, to me, still novel. It is one of the handicaps with which I am still painfully grappling: the sad, sinful impoverishment of South African whites. Their deliberate spiritual dehydration and moral blindness.

It cannot have been easy for Lindy to refuse the temptation of playing Lady Bountiful to poor, deprived, oppressed us. Many are the hazards white liberals face when reaching out. It is still easy for both the oppressed and those who would alleviate their burden to fall prey to self-defeating patterns of behaviour. At SACHED, one of the first things I learnt was that acknowledging the disadvantages with which I was afflicted didn't excuse me from personal responsibility, especially to myself. No time was wasted on pity: a student's for herself or other people's for her.

At SACHED, though I never heard it said out loud in so many words, our social condition was not acceptable as an excuse for lack of productivity. Pity, self-pity, piteous excuses, just didn't jive with Lindy. And in expecting accountability from us, she taught us self-reliance.

Through tutorials the student assumed some measure of responsibility for her progress. SACHED provided the wherewithal, including the physical accommodation, books, fees, access to the library of the University of Cape Town; the encouragement of peer support, discussion groups, films; and the challenge of divergent political opinion, the peculiarities, prejudices, and pertinent insights we brought to SACHED because of who we were, what we were officially classified as, and what that meant to us about ourselves and about others classified differently.

I found a very small group of highly motivated, bright young students when I joined SACHED: Farieda Khan, Zubeida Desai, Rachmat Omar, all much younger than I was. They were studying for the GCE. There were men students but only Abubakar Solomons, who came later, belongs to what I consider my SACHED group: the group who were present at the last scene of my father's life.

SACHED was a true alloy, a mini melting-pot. It represented an ethnic amalgam, bringing together differently classified people who would not otherwise have met. The SACHED experience was a great leveller. One's social standing within whatever group you were locked into by law had no bearing on one's studies and the attainment of one's goals.

It was here that I later met African women from Guguletu, Langa, and Nyanga. Some, like me, were teachers. But for one or another reason, we had never met. Or if we had, we had found no need, no urge, to connect.

I had met Kuku January briefly when we were both students. Our lives, until SACHED, had never really crossed. From afar, I had heard of her doings, caught a dazzling glimpse of her at some teachers' meetings.

At SACHED, Kuku and I became such good friends that

today we call each other *Sithandwa*, Beloved. I have still not quite recovered from the amazing discovery that Kuku and other people like her can actually find me attractive as a friend.

Where had I learnt that the beautiful, the brilliant, the moneyed had no use for the likes of me who am none of these things?

Soon after I became one of its students, SACHED broadened its scope and admitted UNISA students. Kuku and Nozipho Ngele, née Sono, were UNISA students. The idea that I might do university studies, in South Africa moreover, was novel to me. I would not have been doing the GCE had I even thought of this option. One, let me hasten to add, that I didn't immediately embrace. Others could study through UNISA. Others had better brains, obviously.

Nozipho and Kuku are the main reason I hold a degree from UNISA. Yes, I did not go to England for my degree. And I am the richer, I believe, for the experience.

Today, thanks to these two women, my knowledge of my mother tongue may not be that of a Jolobe or a Mqhayi, but compared with what it was up to the time I left Bantu Education, qualified to teach it, I have now reached the mountain tops, linguistically speaking.

Maybe I am not as shy as I believe I am. For it was I who initiated our first meaningful encounter, not Kuku with all the confidence I believed was hers by virtue of her great beauty, nor Nozipho. I approached these two people, believing they were way above me and not likely to be interested in knowing my name.

We were sitting at adjacent tables – I, mulling over some baffling question of history when I overheard these two ladies commiserate over their disastrous Xhosa paper. Soon, not only was I listening to their perplexed utterances, I could see the solution to their problems. I was convinced I could help.

If I got nothing else from the GCE course, I would still be

grateful for learning appreciation of literature for the first
time in my long school life. Many are the prescribed books,
Xhosa, English, and Afrikaans, I had waded through at
school without ever seeing, without gleaning any learning
whatsoever, any beauty or structure, any theme. I would be
lying if I said that my eye was ever drawn to appreciation of
beauty, rhyme, word, subtlety, phrase, or meaning. We did
not get beyond the vague, general outline of the story, the
who, when, where aspects.

Those two poor souls had only studied through the
Department of Bantu Education. Now UNISA demanded of
them an appraisal of Xhosa literature.

With some hesitancy, I offered my help:

'I'm not sure,' I ventured, 'but I hear what you say;
although I don't know much Xhosa, I have done some crit-
ical appreciation of English literature...'

After some discussion we agreed that the principles had
to be the same. They were more than willing to give it a
shot. Their grades left them eager to try anything, accept
help from any source. Both were doing exceedingly well in
grammar. But they were certain they would not get the sub-
minimum in the literature paper. And that spelt *fail*.

That day my sizzling love affair began with my language.
That day too began my friendship with both women. Later I
would introduce Nozipho to her future husband.

The very next year I was doing Xhosa I through UNISA.
As I unravelled the literature side of the language, these two
women removed the curtain of darkness that had always
obscured the grammar of my language. O happy day – that I
opened my mouth, and offered to help two women I
thought were too stuck-up to give me even the time of day!

Much, much later, when we were so at ease with each
other that showing our pimples was no calamity, imagine
my surprise and disbelief when they told me:

'You were so curt with us, civil and correct, we thought
you were a snob.'

I was flabbergasted. My carefully nursed shyness, real and painful to me, is not as obvious to others as I thought it was. I am still learning this truth, because unfortunately this was not the last time I was to hear this unlikely accusation levelled at me.

The Xhosa venture was a spectacular success. I got a distinction in the end-of-the-year exams. SACHED made me a tutor for Xhosa literature in the Xhosa I, II and III courses, although I only have Xhosa I. And it was a labour of love.

Wherever two or more are gathered, I believe, one will always find misunderstandings, jealousies, and hurts: real or imagined. SACHED was no exception. But there was a special spirit that drew the most unlikely people together.

If ministers are highly respected, their wives who *ex officio* head the women's *Manyano* [Union] are even more elevated. I don't pretend to understand why this is so. But it is.

Mrs Tetiwe, a teacher at the Langa High School and a minister's wife, came to SACHED, and I discovered in her the ordinary human being that lurks within each person whatever trappings may camouflage it. We studied History together, MaDlamini and I; and many are the jokes I have heard from her lips. Without the SACHED experience, we would still be strangers, names to each other at best.

Mrs Grace Qunta, whose passing away I have recently learned of with sadness, changed drastically in my eyes as a result of our interaction at SACHED. Society had, deservedly let me add, put her in the lofty echelons. A highly accomplished, sophisticated lady, a woman of substance in Cape Town and South Africa as a whole and, indeed, beyond that country's borders, I got to know her at SACHED in a way not otherwise possible.

We had a running joke between us. Mrs Qunta's mother was a woman of my clan, a MamTolo. Mother is of her clan, MaDlamini. Clearly, one of us had to address the other as aunt, or *makazi* (mother's sister). I asserted that she, older and therefore birthed by my clan before I was by hers, ought to pay homage. To this silliness Grace, eyes twinkling, retorted:

'*Wethu, ndimdala kuwe. Nguwe omawuthi Makazi kum.* Hey you, I'm older than you. It is you who should say aunt to me.' Her mother, Grace would add, could never have had a sister my age, while it was conceivable she could be my mother's sister. This, of course, was true.

Grace Qunta and I did English together and, I think, some Psychology courses. On occasion we met at her house to go over material together and help each other. But for the SACHED experience, I really do not see where our paths could have crossed.

Students collaborated, helped each other, and offered each other support and encouragement. But we could not have done it without the generosity of spirit, dedication and sacrifice of the tutors, mostly UCT lecturers, professors and senior students, and other liberals whom Lindy Wilson harnessed. Without their sacrifice, there would have been no SACHED.

As I have said before, we worked hard. But we played even harder. The realities of our harsh lives made it imperative that we learn to laugh at the absurdity of our times. We laughed, for otherwise we would have succumbed, overwhelmed by the gruesomeness of that reality.

Zubeida, a woman of Indian origin, and I were once preparing for examinations. This meant that we were often together at SACHED. We took to scheduling our meal breaks so that they would coincide. We would then go up the road to buy fish and chips or a roll filled with chips.

One Italian shopkeeper must have become intrigued by what he perceived as a rather unusual friendship: an Indian woman and an African woman not in a mistress–maid relationship – women displaying ease, familiarity and, yes, friendship and camaraderie. It was too much for this man. One day he could contain himself no more. His curiosity got the better of him and he ventured, 'Are you two sisters?'

'No. We are brothers!' replied Zubeida promptly while I was still dumbfounded, too shocked by such blatant racism to gather my wits and give an appropriate response.

Are you two sisters? Sounds innocent enough, doesn't it? But, of course, that is not what this man was really asking. His hidden question was: What is an Indian woman doing with an African woman? How can you two be friends? How dare you break the carefully demarcated boundaries of this society? Why are you not observing and maintaining your different identities and the painstaking classification the government has devised for you?

To Zubeida's retort, the man cried out, 'You got me!' And as soon as the two of us were out of that shop I couldn't keep the tears of laughter from running down my cheeks – convulsions shaking my body like a leaf – hearing such sarcasm, sharp as a farmer's shears, from Zubeida, my petite and mild-mannered friend.

It seemed to me that most fisheries in the Cape Peninsula were run by Italians or Portuguese. But wherever they had come from, it had to be where there are less than a dozen black people in the entire country. What bothered me was the attitude some seemed to have towards Africans. Their too-familiar, downright disrespectful ways.

One day I walked into a fish and chips shop on the Main Road in Mowbray. The proprietor was serving a customer. A white person.

'Can I help you?'

'Yes. Fish and chips.'

'Fish and chips. Together?'

'No, separately. Snoek, please.'

'Here. Ninety-five cents.'

'Thank you!'

'Thank you!'

Uncomplicated, simple transaction.

My turn next:

'Yes?' And before I could open my mouth,

'*Kwedini!* [Boy] Here's a *mfazi* [woman] for you!'

I waited to be served.

'*Kwedini!!* Come, you b—' (alluding to the unsavoury character of the 'boy's' mother).

A young African man, who had obviously arrived recently from a village, appeared. The proprietor pointed excitedly to me. The youngster, at least half my age, looked sheepishly at me, awkward and embarrassed. His employer continued goading him.

'*Ungamboyi wena, Sisi. Sisibhanxa esi.*' So saying, the lad left us, disappearing back to where he had come from. Going back to peeling potatoes or whatever these underpaid workers do in the back rooms of fisheries.

I paid for my fish and chips and left the shop. I was strangely consoled by the dignity of that young man. Totally aware of his powerlessness, he had nevertheless refused to be used by his employer.

Had he realised that if he were to abuse me he would be abusing himself? Had he somehow recognised that the man-to-man camaraderie was hogwash? That what his boss was about was racism? I do not know. But that he had been mindful of my feelings, had acknowledged our bond, our custom of respecting age, had not only cheered me. That day it had healed me from the contagion of living among people who taunted us as a matter of course.

'Don't you mind him, *Sisi*. This here is a fool,' he had said.

In the white suburb of Mowbray where SACHED was located, not everyone was exactly thrilled by the idea of black students coming and using their white residential area as if they lived there. To be fair, most of the residents of Mowbray treated us the way white people usually treated black people who, for whatever unfathomable reason, intruded on their turf: with barely concealed intolerance. But there were others, a few, who became professional hecklers.

At that time SACHED rented an upstairs flat from the Christian Institute, and our entrance was at the back of the building. On the opposite side of the little road where one entered were blocks of flats. It was the residents of the flats directly opposite us who were most offended by our presence in Mowbray. And some of them left us in no doubt that they were sorely aggrieved.

One man was particularly vehement in verbalising his protest. In the evenings during the week and for the whole of Saturday and Sunday, he posted himself at a strategic position on the balcony. Hisses, racial epithets and menacing, insulting gestures were his weapons. We ignored him, most of the time.

'Dagga pedlar!' he would yell at a student, especially the few who offended him even more by arriving in their own cars. 'Dagga pedlar! Shebeen queen!' The latter, shouted at well-dressed African women. The whole thing could have been funny were it not so tragic.

'Shebeen queen!' the flaccid-faced man roared at, of all unlikely culprits, Mrs Grace Qunta. This lady was royalty in the townships of Langa and Guguletu. Throughout the entire country she commanded respect and admiration. But to the SACHED neighbours she was vermin.

'Go back to Guguletu! Go back to Langa!' We heard these cries almost daily as we ventured onto unfriendly terrain in pursuit of a dream. We ignored them. We had to ignore them if we wanted education. That is not to say they didn't hurt.

One day, things came to a head. It was evening, and a group of us were leaving the building together. Just outside the gate we stopped to sort out lifts, last-minute arrangements about future meetings, all the things that suddenly crop up after you've discussed everything and are on the way out. Well, before we knew it, a police van zoomed

round the corner. It screeched to a bumpy stop as two
policemen leapt out, banging doors and striding towards us.

At the sight of the police, we'd grown quiet. The balcony
opposite was crawling with spectators, agitators of the spectacle, no doubt. They started yelling, 'They're drunk! Take
them away from here, we want to sleep!' It was a little after
nine. On Saturday.

There were just too many of us to put into the van, so we
trooped up the road to the police station. For some reason, I
was suddenly the spokesperson for the group, demanding
an explanation, threatening legal action, and generally
making the two policemen know they were not going to get
away with what they were doing. Don't ask me how that
would come about, how I would make that happen.

Both men were young, in their early twenties, I'd say.
One of them must have thought the silliness had gone far
enough, that it was time he took charge. He would open a
docket, book us.

Hauling out a formidable-looking ledger from behind the
counter which separated us, he demanded, '*Naam?*' 'Sindiwe
Magona,' I replied and watched him start writing a *C*. I gave
my address and other particulars. But when it came to my
work address, he was so stumped he could not even pretend he wasn't.

I worked at a centre where we helped young school
drop-outs finish high school. The name of the project was
Inxaxheba, which means 'participation'. We hoped to instil
in the students a feeling that they had a role of their own to
play in their education.

'Inxaxheba Study Centre,' I said, not batting an eyelid.

'Whaa-aat!?' And I repeated what I had said.

The policeman looked at me. And I looked right back at
him, 'Aren't you smart' written clearly on my brow. 'Write it
down. Go on, spell it,' I dared the man, without once opening my black lips that could speak his tongue as well as my
own.

He was not about to stoop that low. He had a duty to uphold his status.

'GET OUT! GET OUT OF HERE!' The man was livid.
Gnarled roots of ancient trees stood out where his veins
should have fed his temples. 'OUT!' he roared, murder in his
eyes. The rest of the group had been told to wait outside.
The Mowbray police station was a small one-room affair
and, no doubt, the two officers didn't feel like being
swamped by our blackness.

'You dragged me here, if you remember,' I retorted, saun-
tering towards the door.

Outside, the others were howling with laughter, for the
whole thing *was* ludicrous. But, as if we needed it, this
episode was a sobering reminder of just how precarious our
lives were.

Writing now, remembering the time of these episodes,
reminds me of another that happened to me.

I had arranged to meet my son on the first floor of a
department store in Adderley Street, Cape Town.

I saw him coming up the escalators. As soon as he
stepped off, I propelled him to the flight going down.

We were leaving the basement when a heavy, decidedly
hostile hand grabbed me by the scruff of the neck.

Surely, I thought to myself, this is a friend, someone who
hasn't seen me for years, a little too enthusiastic perhaps.

I turned. The stony face looking at me never had been
my friend. He looked less amicable than a mother puffadder
with day-old baby snakes and, if his demeanour was anything to go by, even if we were the only shipwrecked
survivors on a desert island he would never be my friend.

I had to take a stand. People were staring. A crowd had
begun forming.

'Let go of me! I have ears, you know? Tell me what you
want!'

'Come back into the store.'

'Why?'

'Never mind why. Just come.'

I bridled. My son was standing near me with a look on his face of confusion, anger, and something else I couldn't lay my finger on.

'Come!' said the man pulling me by the arm.

'I'll come if you'll let me walk by myself. You're not dragging me anywhere,' I threatened, not quite knowing how I'd execute my threat.

Several female security guards had by this time surrounded us.

We walked back into the store and towards the lifts, my son at my side. The man who had accosted me tried to bar my son from entering the lift.

'He is coming,' I snarled. 'I am not yet in jail, you know. He's coming.'

I was putting up a convincing act. The man stepped aside, and Sandile and I and what looked like a troop of security guards and other store employees went into the lift. Doors closed. Our man pressed the top-floor button.

'You'll be sorry for this,' I hissed. I was sorry at that very moment.

I wondered miserably who, of the people who had just witnessed this, knew me. I was ashamed, I realised. Ashamed and angry. Very angry because I already knew the outcome: a big fat nothing would follow my humiliation. I'd trudged down this muddy lane before.

A twinge of doubt unseated my confidence. Right out of nowhere, it came, attached its tentacles onto my guts, sucking and gnawing. My sense of innocence took flight, deserting me. What, I asked myself, if unbeknown to me, someone had planted stolen property in my bag?

The half hour or so I had killed browsing around on the first floor began to assume an ominous shade in the light of the nightmare of the now: I'd bumped into several people, former students and colleagues I had not seen for years. Of these people, who might be suspect?

A kaleidoscopic parade of faces blurred in my mind as I tried to pick the likely culprit. Lost to me was the irony of myself, almost in handcuffs, going on a mental witch-hunt, trying to find a thief among people I knew.

As the lift stopped, doors sliding open, my heart clogged. This is it! I told myself, following the cluster directing me.

A door swung open. Never again will I ask, 'How does a condemned man walk to the electric chair?'

'This is Mr Van der Merwe, our manager,' or words to that effect.

'Please, sit down,' commanded the manager. Gratefully, I sank into a chair. My knees had gone on unscheduled leave.

'Please, open your bag!' From the same man.

'Would someone please tell me what this is about?'

I had, miracle of miracles, found my voice! But even as this slice of sanity appeared, a ball of worms in the pit of my stomach sent a searing impulse:

'Bargain! If you don't waste their time they'll be lenient!' whispered a small voice from the depth of my trepidation.

The bag I was carrying was big enough to stash quite a lot in, and then some more. I fumbled with the zip, hands unwilling to cooperate. Eyes filled. Focus hazed. My throat was lined old parchment.

The bag revealed itself devoid of everything except what I recognised.

The relief of a Barabbas washed through me. Tears coursed down my face. I forgot all about my son!...

When I recounted this story to friends, all who heard it were dismayed and angry on my behalf. Some even called the manager of this store. I asked a lawyer, a friend's husband, whether I had grounds for a suit.

I got a bouquet of flowers and a letter of apology from the security company. The store also wrote and apologised. Both the store manager and the chief of the security team spoke highly of their man, the training he had received and said perhaps he had been a little over-zealous.

I was assured the security officer had been reprimanded.

The manager invited me to tea in his office and had merchandise that was off-season brought in so that I could select what I needed. Of course, I paid.

Later I received a letter from the lawyer.

Dear Cindi,

Thank you for your letter with enclosures, which I read with great interest.

It is unfortunate and inexplicable that you should have been the victim of two similar incidents both involving this store. I believe this Company to be very concerned with its customer relations and with instilling appropriate attitudes amongst its employees. I have therefore taken the liberty of forwarding the correspondence to the Chairman of the Company for his interest.

Certainly you are at liberty to make whatever use you wish with the correspondence. I think it would be a good idea for you to have a word with the Personnel Director.

It was good to see you again.

I cannot tell you how this letter depressed me, and to this day I am at a loss to figure out what I had expected from this man, the lawyer, my friend's husband, a man who knew me personally. But whatever it was, it surely was not in his letter. I could swallow 'unfortunate', but 'inexplicable' stuck in my throat. As I pondered over how such a brilliant man could have failed to see such an obvious fact, time and time again I was forced to come to the sad conclusion that we were from different worlds, that our frames of reference could not but be dissimilar, and that what was so logical to me was truly 'inexplicable' to him. And for a sound reason. He had no experience of being treated, *always,* like a leper, and I had. And the memory of that treatment ordered my re-action to how others treated me. I knew, even as a child knew, that racism was the reason I 'should have been the victim of two similar incidents' from that shop and an incalculable number of others from elsewhere in the country.

The distinction here is that what the lawyer sees as two isolated incidents is anything but that; it is our daily bread. And it was this failure to recognise that fact which left me so chagrined. But then, as they say, you gotta miss it if you ain't at da boat stop. And the lawyer and people like him are miles from the boat stop.

Ten

And then the very air in the country began to change. Things began to stir. Disquiet befell the whole land. Black people were disgruntled. There was nothing remarkable about that. They had long been disgruntled. As far back as memory could recall, for centuries black people had been disgruntled in South Africa. But now? Now they were voicing their discontent. Openly.

Growing up, I had come to a gradual, reluctant realisation of our collective disgruntlement. Now black people were saying out loud, boldly, that they had been robbed of their land, they had been deprived of their rights.

Now they were saying that they were being robbed of their soul as thousands upon thousands set forth each day to the factories and to the farms, to the mines and to the offices, into the white homes, sweeping the streets by day and spending their nights watching over the wealth housed in the safes inside the buildings at whose steps they sat warming their hands over the flames of the crude braziers.

Now they were demanding part of that wealth. They were tired of driving big executives who rushed across the country making big money.

They were sick of waiting for the crumbs that white South Africa dared label wages. They were done, they said, mending broken bodies for a third of the salary of others doing the same.

They denounced going to school to be trained to be nothing by teachers who had gone through hell and were still there.

They declared that each day they were paying, each with a little piece of his life, each paying the unforgivable, inescapable sin of being black.

I heard them and agreed with what they were saying publicly. I had heard it all before. For a long time it had been said. Only, until now, it had been whispered privately.

They raised the issue that those black bodies worked hard, killing themselves for enough so that they would be there on the morrow – to be killed a little once more.

The air of disquiet could be felt in the black ghettos, the segregated townships where Africans were forced to live. It could be felt in the segregated townships where coloured people lived apart. Even those who had managed somehow to escape into the plush residential areas set aside for middle-class coloured people could feel it. The Indian community felt it in their legally designated residential areas. It even seeped into the usually impervious residential areas where only people born white could live.

My people, AmaXhosa, say that when quails take flight a storm is brewing: I witnessed committees spring up; one after the other they mushroomed. This one was for reconciliation, that over there for peace and justice. There were those committees whose aim it was to have black people work their problems out exclusively of whites. There were white committees working to strengthen the white position which they felt threatened. There were women's groups and there were youth groups, church groups and secular groups, political groups, non-political groups and apolitical groups. They sprang up all over the land.

It was a time of great activity. Exciting. Frightening. And all-embracing.

Writers wrote columns in daily newspapers and articles in magazines. They wrote books too. Academia became prolific in speech-giving, in lecturing, in seminar-organising, data collection and survey-conducting.

Prose, poetry and drama flourished: it was generally

agreed that the burning question was the reordering of our society. The stumbling block? The sacrifices no one was willing to make.

Black people said everything had been taken from them and they would no longer sacrifice.

White people, accustomed to everything being given to them, took more as their right and saw no good reason to throw away any of the much they had.

There had been stirrings before in the land. The government did not blink an eyelid. It had found ways of quelling them. It announced it was ready for any mischief.

Disquiet grew to fervour. The fervour grew and in the second half of the year 1973 it swallowed up even me: I became, quite by accident, a member of Church Women Concerned. CWC marked a turning-point in my life.

In this group I met women who were white – not white women. I met women who were classified coloured – not coloured women. I met women of Indian descent. For the first time in my life, in my thirtieth year, I encountered people – *yes*, with a different colour skin, but they were people first.

They spoke with me, person to person. We shared ourselves. They listened to what I had to say. I, in turn, heard what they said.

We broke bread together. We prayed together. We sang together. At night, we shared cubicles and used the same bathrooms, taking showers in the morning. We took walks, talked, laughed and anguished over the sad stupid blight blanketing the land we all called home.

At a time when including a person classified other than oneself in one's circle of friends was an event of uncommon rarity, CWC provided a means of correcting that deficiency. Even Cape Town, reputedly of liberal tradition, had few people who could boast relationships across the colour line. Relationships not of the master–servant kind, that is.

I discovered human beings in these white women and,

through them, in their families.

Church Women Concerned was the brainchild of Shirley Turner, a white woman whose humanity somehow transcended that liability. Like most of the women I was to encounter in this group, Shirley had been groping for another way, a better way, different from the country's 'traditional way of life'. A Methodist, she had been sent by her church to an international conference in Greece.

There she had been forced to confront not only the issues of her home country, South Africa, but also the fact that she belonged to the oppressor class. That whether or not she supported the laws of the land, the segregation of the races, the oppression of the darker people of her country, was an aside. The overriding factor was the inescapable privilege her white skin accorded her.

At the end of the conference each participant had had to come up with a proposal for a project that would address itself to a problem which the home church faced. Shirley's had been Church Women Concerned.

I had become involved with this group by a stroke of luck. Grace Qunta, who had been asked to organise the African contingent, had been let down by those she had asked. She came to me on the morning of the event, and I, tongue in cheek, agreed to go and spend a whole weekend with a group of women, women I did not know. And, as if that wasn't bad enough, I had to bring a Bible! I couldn't think of a better recipe for thorough, undiluted boredom. In fact, had this lady asked me in time, I would certainly have declined. That's human nature for you. I even believed she had not thought me good enough to ask when she had asked the others. But the poor woman was almost in tears. I could just imagine her dilemma: here she is, the vital link between CWC and her people … and, typically, she fails them. So I felt a little sorry for her. And unlike most women she knew, I didn't have to ask my husband whether I could go. I may not have agreed to do this for the right reasons, but thank God I did.

Of necessity, the opportunity thus created was artificial. However, it could not have been otherwise, for South Africa legally prohibited socialising between the races and put numerous obstacles in the way of such contact.

CWC enabled us, as women in that part of South Africa, to see ourselves as ordinary citizens who found themselves in decidedly far from ordinary circumstances. In truth, some of us were not even considered citizens, strictly speaking: the African had, by this time, been completely deprived of that privilege.

The self-exploration and discussions that we, members of CWC, embarked on stunned and shocked us. We realised that not only were we law-abiding, we had become zealots in this respect, without even trying.

We were leagues ahead of the restrictive legislation of our beloved country. Whilst decrying the present legal system, we had done better than it intended, for we found that we even kept laws that had not as yet been enacted.

Our analysis, painful and astounding to ourselves, led us to the realisation that we had become who we were, by law:

Had we not gone to school, by law? Had we not lived in areas set aside for us, by law? Had we not married men of our own race, as the law stipulated? Borne children of the same race as we were? Sent them to school with like-skinned children, again as the law told us to do? Worshipped the same God in legally segregated places of worship, as the law deemed fit?

In illness had we not been admitted, without a murmur from us, to hospitals or wards exclusively 'ours' by race? And in death, we knew we would be put to rest with our own kind. That was the law, and we observed it to the letter. And more.

We smiled only at those who looked like us when no law existed that forbade smiles across the colour line. What if the law said a white hostess could not have a party where liquor would be served if there was an African guest? Who had ever said liquor was the party?

Sex across the colour line was forbidden. True. But friendship wasn't. Restaurants were closed to Africans and coloured people. They were 'whites only'. So were most cinemas. All the better beaches too. Trains, buses and taxis were segregated also. Lavatories, at work and in public places, of course. But the shops weren't (although some progressive element of the white right wing had proclaimed this a legal flaw). The mountain wasn't. Private cars weren't. Church halls weren't. And much more.

In CWC, because we wanted to come together, we found ways of being together. Some of these were marginally legal to be sure, but most were perfectly above board.

Why, we wondered, had we not seen these possibilities before? Impatiently, we burned fervently, praying for others to convert to our way of thinking.

Why wouldn't they see that they would be far happier having shed the stupid, onerous burden of maintaining 'correct' relations between the races?

As might be surmised, CWC was multi-racial, multi-denominational, inclusive of all faiths. It had members from the Christian faith, the Islamic faith and the Jewish faith. The primary objective was to build bridges, to effect reconciliation, to attempt to live lives that projected well into the future, to a time when the laws that separated us according to skin colour would be no more.

It was a fond dream put forward as a testimony of faith. We truly believed the possibility existed for apartheid to be dismantled. Therefore, it behoved us to hasten the process by living the future in the now.

Action: speakers' groups were formed. The word had to be spread. We went from home to home, from church to church. We went to mosque and synagogue. We went to schools and centres of higher learning. We went to sports organisations. We were afire.

Even the groups we sent out on speaking engagements demonstrated what we stood for: always three women went – one coloured, one white and one African. The talks were well planned and thoroughly rehearsed, with some members standing in for the audience. They were executed with precision, our fervent belief firing our tongues, freeing us of all inhibition, shyness or reticence. Missionaries among heathens had no greater driving force.

Until I became a member of CWC, I had thought rarely of white people. And on the rare occasion my mind would occupy itself with such a gainless exercise, the thoughts were seldom complimentary. Whites were happy. They were carefree. They were spoilt. They were rich. They had everything. In short, they were all I wasn't. Overwhelmed by my lack of options, I looked upon their pass-free world, a world filled with choice, as paradise.

It seems strange now, of course, but the idea of, say, white people suffering bereavement never crossed my mind. Even their tragedies were so far removed from my world that I had never stopped to think of white people doing anything they didn't choose to do. How was I to begin thinking that people like that might be hurt sometimes?

To me, until then, hurt was poor. Hurt was hungry. Hurt was unemployment. Hurt was being denied the right to be in a particular urban area. Hurt was illness with no money for a doctor's visit. Hurt was losing all your worldly belongings in a tin-shack fire. Hurt was a mother carrying the dead body of her baby on her own back, steeling herself not even to whimper because doing so might lead to detection and then she would not be allowed onto the bus that would take her back to the village she had left that morning, hoping against hope that the white doctor in town would be able to save her baby. She knows the regulations: she should hire a car. But she does not have that kind of money. So she would not acknowledge her grief, her loss, until it was convenient to do so.

To me, hurt was the door crashing open, in the middle of the night, torches piercing bright into the eyes, policemen demanding passes to see that all those sleeping in that house had the right to be there.

Hurt, to me, was being told, by billboards announcing a coming theatre attraction:

'No Person under 19! No Dogs, and No Bantu!'

The Bantu was me and all African people.

Hurt was a white train-conductor asking a colleague of his, *'Wat soek hierdie ding hier?* What does this thing want here?'

The thing was me. I had inadvertently clambered onto a 'Whites Only' coach, the train pulling out, my coach two hundred metres down the platform.

Hurt was the Dairy Board's promotion slogan, 'Do you love your children? ... Give them butter!', when I was hard pressed putting together enough money for half a loaf of bread. And the Meat Board did not help. It had a jingle that seemed to be posted on every bus I was on:

Prime Meat is Best.

Super Meat is Next by Test.

Grade One is known as Good.

Grade Two will serve as Food.

Grade Three will Hunger Satisfy.

That hit hard. Especially on a day when I was feeling good about having scraped enough to afford tripe, spleen or other innards for the children and myself. Hurt! What did white people know about it? They had choice. This one right denied me all my life was theirs by virtue of their skin.

It had never occurred to me that even thus born, qualified for choice, white South Africa might encounter hardship. Who chooses misery? Who but a madman would choose unhappiness over bliss, misfortune over fortune, disappointment over fulfilment, despair over hope?

Since white people were in charge of their lives as well as mine, I truly believed they would not stint on themselves the care they so lavished on me. My ignorance or knowledge of whites – yes, even that – can be put at their doorstep: it is the direct result of choice. Their choice! Their choice to separate people with such success that we might as well have lived in different countries, for all we know about each other, about ourselves.

In CWC there was a lot of learning for white women about the experience of black women. Black women had their lessons too. For me a whole strange world opened. What I had known about whites paled against what I began to glimpse, to suspect, to learn.

CWC set out to recruit women perceived as being in positions of leadership in their own communities. Through these women, the aim was to reach their families, friends, neighbours and their associates. Eventually, it was hoped the ripple would affect the wider society. Specifically, attitude change was the ultimate objective. The *modus operandi* was simple, extraordinary only for taking place at that time, in South Africa where such events assumed qualities of political daring. A group of women, carefully selected so that the composition would reflect an even distribution with regard to religion, denomination, creed and colour, would spend a weekend together, away from their families and their friends.

Issues pertaining to religion, politics and society would be explored. Mildly confrontational, the group dynamics were set up in such a way that most women felt safe. Even the name, Church Women Concerned, had been chosen with this in mind. For if nothing else, white South Africa perceives itself as Christian.

Under the broad umbrella of religion, therefore, each woman was led into a journey inward, then outward, and finally these two spheres came together. The women were made to feel secure enough for each to assume personal responsibility for her thoughts and actions, her beliefs and her attitudes. The interaction, encouraged by participation in very small groups, led to an openness few had experienced before.

Together, we looked at the law of man, contrasted it with the law of God, examined how, as believers, we had lived out our very ordinary lives. Most of us came to see that in obeying man's law, the law of the land, we had transgressed that of our Creator.

Readings from the various faiths were used. From these discussions ensued. Women who had thought of themselves as devout became appalled when challenged about their response to what almost everyone agreed was a sinful state of affairs, the scandal of apartheid.

As individuals, we saw we were all caught up in its far-reaching tentacles, be it in the soul-destroying, same-looking, individuality-lacking ghettos of the disfranchised or in the soul-destroying, decadent splendour of ill-gotten wealth.

White women could not escape the privilege which their colour bestowed on them. Black women could not escape the discrimination theirs made them heir to.

We were all brought face to face with the faceless 'them' we had known, without knowing, all our lives! All of us were made to face our acquiescence: 'For evil to flourish, it is enough for good people to do nothing' ran one of our slogans. We could have crumbled in the face of the guilt we came to feel. We did not allow ourselves that route out. It is one particularly favoured by white South Africans. We were forced to go beyond the beating of our chests, beyond wallowing in self-pity or remorse, beyond despairingly shrugging off apartheid and its results, beyond allowing feelings of helplessness to overwhelm us.

Very capable group facilitators took us beyond that to a point where we felt we had some kind of control. The emphasis was on the assumption by the individual woman of responsibility for becoming an agent for change. We saw that we could have an input into the direction the country would take and was even then taking: pain and helplessness gave way to optimism. Or was it euphoria?

I would like to think that in the more than five years of this group's existence I was able to help at least one white woman forget the black in black people! For the tragedy of South Africa is rooted in our having preconceived notions about other groups. Whites know blacks. Blacks know whites. Those classified coloured know Africans and they are known to us. We know so much of groups that the individuals in those groups are completely lost to us. Faceless.

I am an African and I have never dared make that claim with reference to the indigenous South African people, over twenty million souls: each unique; each having undergone countless experiences, some of which may not even be accessible to the individual's memory; each a singular expression of the love of God – yes, even the African. And would I have the temerity to profess to know these millions? Who am I? Knowing a group inevitably leads to focusing on what is perceived in that group as different. And worse, it leads to stereotyping.

It is precisely this kind of knowledge that not only denies the inherent individuality of all persons, but also blinds us to the similarities among all people, similarities greater in number and weight than the differences.

I had not known the depth and strength of this knowledge about me that white South Africa holds, till I was confronted with questions such as, 'What do your people want?' And this from the liberal white, the white who professed enlightenment, who said whites and blacks should talk, should get to know one another; not the diehard, conservative Afrikaner.

This question and similar ones spoke volumes of the distance, the barrier between the questioner, white, and me, black:

'What do your people want?' not only makes the false assumption that I, because of the colour of my skin, know the needs of all other people coloured as I am. It also assumes that the questioner, being of different colour, doesn't, couldn't and will never know these needs.

That we are people is of no importance as a basis for comparison. We, black, have needs that must be different: thus blinded by his assumption, the person sees no common ground between us.

Colour, an attribute, has been mistaken for quality, the essence.

In the desert of South Africa's traditional way of life, CWC was an oasis, artificial of necessity but courageous by virtue of its very existence. For the participants it was a joyful, painful event; exciting, extraordinary, an expression of rare collective optimism in that land.

Rooted in the conviction that people were capable of change, CWC was an acknowledgement of human intelligence which, given favourable conditions, will flourish. We willed this intelligence to break down stereotypes. We put faith in the ability of women to be agents for social change.

I remember the first weekend. Accommodation had been found at a Catholic convent. There were legal problems regarding African women sleeping over, and we had to be ferried back into the townships at night.

For subsequent weekends (we never gave them a formal label such as encounters or seminars) we did not have to go through this exercise, having obtained legal opinion that we could spend the night under one roof. The weekends ran from late afternoon on Friday, straight after work, to Sunday afternoon tea.

We spent the time in prayerful reflection, working in small groups but sometimes meeting in a plenary session as a single group.

We, the participants, brought up what issues we felt pertinent, be they personal or family-related, issues concerning relations between husband and wife or between black and white, white and coloured, coloured and African. These were examined, analysed and discussed.

There were disagreements and there were revelations. Women revealed their deprivation, for we all found we had been moulded by the same craftsman. Yes, even white women discovered that they had led lives filled with illusions in materially comfortable and spiritually arid splendour.

There was a lot of pain in our joyful discovery of each other and of ourselves.

For the black woman, this befriending of whites was a risky business on two counts: the government kept a hawk-like eye on people who stepped beyond the prescribed limits. And black people were far more vulnerable, easier to molest and terrorise, crush and kill! Their lives, in the government's assessment, were cheaper than a whistle.

On the other hand, township dwellers viewed befriending 'them', the oppressors, as flirting with danger. Wasn't the natural next step 'selling out'? Unshakable self-knowledge of one's innocence can thin before the guilt born of collective condemnation.

The white women, I am sure, had their crosses to carry: lack of support, if not downright opposition, from family, church or friends. They could be seen as traitors and kaffir-lovers by *verkrampte* whites.

But our own glad awakening to our wealth anchored us. Our spirits soared. Our minds focused with ferocious determination. Strengths, hitherto unsuspected, emerged from some of the members. I discovered that I was good at facilitating small groups. I also uncovered some of my own prejudices about other groups, to say nothing of enormous ignorance.

Until I met Sylvia Collier, Bellville was in my mind a place peopled with *verkrampte* whites, a close second behind Paarl and Stellenbosch, the stronghold of beyond-redemption reactionary whites.

Sylvia was not only of English stock, she was Catholic and very, very progressive in her political outlook. My Bellville theory flew out the window. What is more, the foundation cracked, and I began doubting the accuracy of my hitherto unquestioningly accepted beliefs. Not just about Bellville either.

In this group a realisation of our ability to love someone belonging to another group, someone of a different skin colour, took place. 'We have a lot in common.'

I had never heard those words said to me by a white person before, and when a coloured person said them they would invariably be referring to our oppression by white people. I certainly would never have thought of saying such words to a white person, and even if I had, I would not have dared. The thought would have appeared impertinent. To harbour such a thought would have alarmed me into asking myself: Sindiwe, who do you think you are?

As I've said, pain and being white had never connected in my mind. After joining CWC I was to learn of white hurt: childlessness, marital infidelity, problem children, health problems, alcoholism, divorce, loss of faith, guilt about the situation in the country, fear for sons reaching the age when the military would call them up to serve their country, debt, and a host of others.

Okay, so some of these problems were different from those plaguing the women of my world or, where similar, the emphasis was different. These women had jobs or else their husbands made enough to free them from the necessity of working. Their children would never suffer from malnutrition. They lived in what looked like castles. But was their pain any less? I couldn't say. Not when I got down to the harsh, brutal question: How does one measure pain?

I stood confounded by the same question, over and over, when coloured and African oppression was compared. Were coloured people less oppressed because more was given to them than had been given to Africans? Coloured people did not carry passes. They had better houses which they could even own. Their salaries, while not equal to the salaries of whites, were far above what Africans earned. However, coloured people were not fully fledged citizens in South Africa.

Much later and in another context, I would be confounded by the same stratification of human suffering among the country's Africans. Whilst it is acknowledged that we all have suffered under apartheid, there seems to be a school of thought that propounds the belief that those who have never been jailed have not really suffered. And even among those who have been jailed, 'graduates' of Robben Island rank a higher notch – they have suffered the most. Trust me to miss the obvious. Of course, there are glaring cases: Nelson Mandela, sentenced to life in prison, served twenty-seven years of that sentence. His case is an example of extreme suffering. But I would never say that he began suffering only after he was locked up in jail. I fail to see why he would have risked so much had he been happy. It is his suffering and the suffering of his people that led him to take the steps he took. Call me a simpleton, but weighing human pain baffles me no end.

Tell me, who bleeds more? The coloured called Hottentot or the African called Kaffir? Questions such as these assailed and confronted me as I plunged myself into the task of building bridges. Later I became a member of the committee administering CWC. I helped in the recruitment drive. Other women, also classified Bantu, came to be members. I helped arrange and run weekends. I forged personal links, some of which have survived the test of time and lasted to this day.

As in all families, however, it was not roses all the way. We and our families visited each other's homes. When our white friends came in their unbattered cars we were so scared someone would take off in them, it was hard concentrating on or enjoying their visit.

Our lack of the luxuries taken for granted in their own homes was sharpened by their mere presence: where would they go should they have need to relieve themselves? My own toilet, a good thirty metres away from my back door, was inaccessible in winter when the whole back yard was under water; I do not now and did not then have a boat! White people are always washing hands. That is quite okay when you have the wherewithal for that. I lived minus hot water, minus bathroom and minus electricity. I had one sink, in the kitchen.

When we went visiting white homes, admiration vied with envy. That left the black sister feeling bad for having such unsisterly and uncharitable thoughts. To suppress those hard feelings of guilt, we would then diminish the importance of the relationship to us: what sister would let another live in the squalor in which I live? Also, we reminded ourselves that those women owed us nothing.

But we had this searing vision of a South Africa that had turned around. Where the very diversity of its people was its source of strength, its wealth, its joy and its hope, instead of its scourge.

Sisterhood forged ahead. Bonds strengthened. So bright was the mirage that it blinded us. After several years of very hard work we had created a warm, safe place, unique and rare, precious: a sizeable group of people, friends with bonds of caring, admiration, patience, understanding and love.

Such a group, made up of women of such differing backgrounds, is an event rarer than gold in South Africa.

We were attempting to move a mountain with our bare hands. After some time the hands began to bleed. We used the sinews, raw muscle, tendons and bone that showed through the skinless hands. The reward was great, the pain greater.

Members moved away from Cape Town as the needs of their families and their own lives dictated. Some went abroad, some went elsewhere within the country, others moved from one Cape Town suburb to another.

The pass laws made it illegal for the African to move from

one urban area to another. Those of us thus locked in the ghettos we couldn't escape seethed with anger as our helplessness was highlighted by these 'never-for-us' activities. However, such was the absurdity of our lives that we were forced to fight fiercely to keep even what we so hated. Yes, I did resent that as an African I had no mobility.

Our sisters in CWC, to whom that freedom of movement was no novelty or crying for the moon, could have no way of knowing the unsisterly feelings they provoked in some of us when they exercised that right. (Surely it couldn't just have been me?)

'How could she move so far away from me? She knows I have no car. What was wrong with her palace in —? She was so accessible then, and I could go to her house. In fact, I had a standing invitation to come for a bath any day I wanted.

'Yes, maybe that is why she is running away to —. I don't care how nice her new house is. I will never go there. She can keep it. I will never put my foot in that house of hers.'

Such a (silent) tirade would be followed by contriteness. Disbelief and confusion. What had come over me? What made me think people should ask for my permission before they moved or consider the inconvenience to me when deciding the location of their new home? White people?

Of course, there was also the realisation, in instances like this, that we were hitting at those white people who were moved to do something about the unholy political order in our country. The ones we would have truly liked to throttle, the ones who believed we have tails, the ones who saw themselves as our masters and our gods – those whites were in no danger of being abused by the likes of me.

Eleven

1976. A year that dawned full of promise. As a family, we entered the teens: Thembeka turned thirteen, on 4 January.

I was absolutely abustle that month. I had been invited to the International Women's Tribunal on Crimes Against Women, to be held in Brussels early that year. One of two delegates from South Africa, I would be sponsored by women from the Scandinavian countries.

The other delegate was my friend Anne Mayne. Anne could not believe what I had to go through before I could get on that plane.

As a white South African, Anne's application for a passport was a mere formality. Imagine her growing horror as she witnessed my amazing marathon. To get the application form on which to apply for a passport, I had first to pay a five-hundred-rand deposit. So that 'the government can bring you back if you get into trouble overseas', officials informed me. I was not in the habit of getting into trouble. Not once had I been convicted of a crime. And the personal troubles I had brought on myself the government cared naught about and would not have helped me solve even had I been insane enough to seek aid from it. Secondly, when applying for the passport, I was fingerprinted, palmprinted, and all but soleprinted. Then began the gruelling test: 'Next week.' 'Tomorrow.' 'We don't know when Pretoria will send your passport.' 'No news, phone again in a couple of days.'

Those were some of the responses I got each time I went to the offices of the Department of the Interior in Cape

Town. Phoneless in phoneless Guguletu, I had to go there physically to get the astounding news. Meanwhile, while I sweated it out waiting for my passport, the Security Police paid me a visit. It was routine then to inquire about the nature of the trip when an African was going abroad. Who paid for your fare? I've often said the only reason travelling abroad was never legislated against for Africans was that the government realised that given our excuses for salaries we'd never make it.

So those who made it did so because someone else wanted them to, wanted them to do so badly enough to foot the bill. And the government wanted to know why anyone in their right mind, anyone anywhere in this world gone mad, would want one of the pieces of garbage the country was unfortunately saddled with. To find out more about such mad people who would spend their money funding trips by Africans, the government sent the Security Police to dig into the mystery. Where, exactly, were you going? Why? Who were you going to see? Why? Who gave you the money for the trip? Why? What were you going to say about life in South Africa if you were asked?... Seriously, the man from the government sat there, asked questions, recorded responses he felt were of consequence and, after assuring you 'This is just routine', departed. And you were supposed to forget about the whole 'routine' affair, take it as such and go and enjoy yourself overseas, completely relaxed. Why would something 'just routine' intimidate you?

After weeks filled with uncertainty and dread, the day of departure came. And still I didn't have my passport.

The previous day, a Friday, Anne had had the presence of mind to call Pretoria once more. She was told I could pick up the passport at the Department of the Interior in Pretoria.

Without Anne's intervention, I am certain I would not have made it to the conference. Just the physical resources needed to pursue the matter with the Department of the

Interior – the telephone, the money, the time, to say nothing of a conviction-carrying voice, an insistent manner that says, 'You are being absurd. I know what I am talking about' – were out of my reach. I did not have the experience of sounding authoritative and demanding service as a right, and from white civil servants at that. I had grown up learning nothing was mine by right. I had learned that I lived on other people's sufferance.

One word from anything sounding white, however lowly, turned me into a bubbling idiot. Had I had the means and the guts to call Pretoria, one '*Ja?*' or '*Wat soek jy?*' or '*Ons het dit nog nie*' would have pulverised me.

I'd been schooled enough by now to know that mine was not to question but accept my lot. Did Moses ask the voice stupid questions when the flaming bush gave him directives?

Anne and I flew from Cape Town to Johannesburg's Jan Smuts Airport. A friend of Anne's, a teacher at the University of the Witwatersrand, was waiting for us there. He drove us all the way to Pretoria and back to the airport again for the next leg of the trip.

It was midnight when I signed for the receipt of my South African passport and received it from a doorman at the Department of the Interior. Midnight. The women of the Scandinavian countries had provided the money for my ticket, for accommodation, and for my daily needs while at the conference. Well and good. But can you see me ever getting to that conference without the help Anne gave me? She could do for me what no black friend of mine could, because of one thing and one thing only. She is white. White in a country that made that the root of all entitlement. The special grace that belongs to some whites is having realised their privileged position was the reverse side of the same coin that sports black deprivation, and then doing things in their own lives, in little ways, that made a difference here and there without pretending or believing these were solutions to the evil of apartheid. Anne Victoria

Mayne is one such person. And it has been my luck that I have found helping hands along the way as I journeyed forth. People have given me encouragement when my spirits flagged, have bandaged me when I bled, fed me when hungry, shown me the way when I had strayed, held up the mirror so I could see myself. These people, all of them, irrespective of race, sex or class, I call my mothers. Some have even been younger than I am. But I call all of them my mothers, for they have helped me become.

Having never dreamt of seeing the inside of a plane, and having imagined my terror in the unlikely event of ever finding myself there, I remembered just before we landed at Jan Smuts Airport that I was supposed to be scared stiff. However, since I had done so well till then, I saw no reason to change the pleasure filling me.

The Jo'burg stop is a blur of bright city lights, elevated roads, speed, motion. We dashed to Pretoria, received the passport, and then sped back to Johannesburg. The next thing I remember, we are on our way to Brussels. The rest is a blur.

At the conference, I was struck by the range of problems women battle with daily all over the world. So totally enveloped in apartheid had I been, even the concerns of white women whom I happened to know I had perceived through this lens. The overriding issue, the pivot, the essence, was always apartheid. Everything else was seen through it and existed only in its shadow.

My eyes popped out, peeled wider than those of a bullfrog, as painful awareness of the plight of others split the calloused layers around my heart. Incest. Rape. Abuse from men, from women, from government, from family, society, religion, industry, even from those whose very badge stands for life. Colonisation of woman's reproductive organs, belittling of her contribution to humanity, denying her worth. Burdening, badgering, brutalising. And often in such seductive ways.

I listened to the pain as woman after woman testified. Each woman represented a country. Each country, it seemed to me after hearing those cries of the heart, had its own way of making woman suffer.

Even where there was no legal handicapping of women, societal attitudes saw to it that she would remain in a sub-servient role. Some were caught up in a political mess which was not of their making and over which they had little control – women from Israel and the West Bank for instance.

Men made policies the world over. Women suffered consequences. That much became clear to me.

My testimony received a standing ovation. I think, though, that that had less to do with what I said and more with a show of solidarity. I represented the sexual discrimination that was the business of the Tribunal. However, superimposed on this was racial discrimination, the official policy of the government of South Africa: apartheid. The point I attempted to convey was that the African woman was the worst oppressed of all South Africans. Race and sex combined to put her at the bottom of the dung heap, and only her child was more pitiable.

Strategies were formulated. Governments were going to be made more responsive to the needs of women. The feeling was strong that we should keep in touch wherever we were. Knowing that there were others who cared would strengthen and encourage women in their home situations, enable them to go on fighting for their rights. Once more I was enriched and made hopeful. Invigorated. Meeting women from so many countries was intoxicating. Hearing of women's deprivation even in countries I thought of as civilised, progressive, wealthy and developed was disturbing and saddening.

Who said travel broadens? In Belgium I shrunk. I was fine as long as I stayed within the conference. Outside that environment with its simultaneous translation facilities, its sympathetic crowd of feminists and other women, my brain narrowed to a grain of sand as I experienced the absolute horror of total illiteracy. Numbing.

Notices on streets, on entrances to public buildings, near forbidding contraptions, at stations and restaurants, meant nothing at all to poor blind me. *'Sortir'*, *'Entrez,'* these and many more said nought to me. I could not bring meaning to even a single arrangement of letters.

My handicap hurled me back twenty years. The arrogance of those days piled scorn on the me of today. How the sins of a silly teenager visited her in her hour of revelation. I stood naked, head shaven, bereft of even robes of sacking. And the soul of my mocking eyes gave me no reprieve.

Salt River railway station, the scene of my crime, had chalked a living record inside the lids of these scorn-filled eyes of yesteryear. In far-away Brussels, the shabbily clad hordes of African men, straight from village on contract, dogged my every step. Each indecipherable scroll produced a face from the migrant labourers whom we, highly educated students of the Langa High School, had ridiculed. 'Do you know how they know which is the Langa train?' How stupid we'd been, how uneducated and ignorant of our own limitations. We didn't know how the newly arrived migrant was inducted by his kind to find his way home, and saw nothing but backwardness in his endeavours. 'It is a very short word, a word that begins with a pipe. After the pipe, comes a sledge. And the word ends in another sledge' – LANGA. And we, able to differentiate between Langa and Stellenbosch, had found this not only a sign of mental retardation but also highly amusing.

Well, I was far from amused in Brussels. Now I prayed for a similar miracle, a way I could find to read French and feel human and intelligent. Belated admiration for those heroes I'd not known as such flooded my consciousness. How clearly I saw now my undiluted stupidity which I'd never suspected before, as well as the brilliance which those I'd scorned had shown, for what is reading if not gleaning meaning from symbols? Armed with nothing but their God-given wits, their powers of observation and their will to survive, these men dealt with culture shock the best way they knew how. Here I was, with years of study behind me, and I was reduced to a snivelling twit. How true the saying of the Native American, 'Walk in another's moccasins for a full moon before you criticise him.'

The organisers of the conference had left us some time for a little sight-seeing. We also stole the time.

Down long-gone centuries I sallied, admiring with my own eyes the architecture of centuries past, which I had only glimpsed at from stale pages of history books till then.

The Grand Place, resounding with Bach or Beethoven by night, reminded me of the Cape Town Parade by day. Except I had never walked with such abandon at the Parade.

The Musée des Dentelles amazed me with its gay displays of intricate works of lace and brought to mind women from a time long gone, women who had lived their lives as women of my time did, with pain, love, hunger, with tragedy and ecstasy. And still they had found time to make magic with their hands.

At Chez Leon (or was it Au Caleau D'Egmont?) my palate was delighted with mussels, crab meat, and Chateaubriand. Fare available in Cape Town. But who would know of that? Not me, forbidden to enter restaurants in my land. Not me who could not even afford those pleasures.

The Red Light district brought tears to my eyes. Those were somebody's children once upon a time, I thought, startled by the boldness of the new packaging. New in my eyes, that is. I was used to more subtle and stealthy ways, some even bordering on respectability. My pinched Calvinistic morality followed me to a sex shop the next day. As my group wandered about, touching this or that, perhaps even buying something, I, Madonna-like, walked stiffly upright in the middle of the room, away from the displays others fingered, touched or admired. I walked round and found myself, when I looked, with my arms folded. I knew then that I carried the laws of my country with me. I was determined to 'see no evil' right there – in a sex shop. So why had I bothered going in? Voyeurism? I had not known I was such a prude.

Bruges charmed me with its calming canals. Picturesque cobblestones in winding narrow streets spread themselves in warm welcome. I was living in a fairytale. Fairy-godmothers sat outside inviting doors, fingers never still as they wove the magic of their webs.

Then to Ghent I went to meet the messengers who brought the good news long ago. Once more I was a school girl reciting words, never dreaming they'd spring up all real one day.

As I walked up the humble memorial hill at Waterloo, miles of spring meadow brought battle to my heart. Disbelief filled me. How could such carnage have happened on this sleepy, peaceful field that spread itself so innocently today? Was this a lesson, a reminder, of man's inability to assimilate the good all around him?

After the conference I went to London, where my brother Jongi now lived with his family.

I had not seen him for eleven years. The night I spent in Kensington before going to him was the longest night of my life. Anne, who had known Jongi in South Africa, had seen him several times in England and could not understand my impatience. To be that close to him and not see him was hell. I phoned him late that night and we both cried on the phone.

Meaning well, Anne tried to prepare me for disappointment. She reminded me that Jongi and I had not seen each other for years. He had changed, she warned me. I listened, admitting only what I already knew. But when she told me Jongi and his wife might not put me up, I knew we were not talking about the same relationship.

My brother will always have a place for me. Both he and

his wife, I told Anne, would be insulted if I even considered staying at a hotel. Pityingly, Anne looked at me, smiled her sweet and sad smile and quipped, 'Well, my dear, I'm only warning you.'

On the way back, she had the grace to admit, 'You're different. I can't imagine how my sisters or cousins would react if I unexpectedly wanted them to put me up.' Oh, that we had the courage to let such differences enrich us. That was the meaning of Church Women Concerned – celebrating our divergence. Learning from each other. Allowing a cross fertilisation between the vibrant cultures that belong in the country.

My cup was overflowing. The two weeks I spent with my brother and his family just flew. We did not do much, but did we talk! That is when I fell in love with his wife, Nolusapho.

Alone in a strange, cold country, she had helped make a home; they were happy. Their two children, my niece, Elphina Nomfundo, and my nephew, Gerald Jongile, were lovely. I could not but be grateful that she was there loving Jongi.

Jongi had left South Africa as a Rhodes Scholar. We talked about his Oxford days, his experiences working and living in London, his teaching (which he was then busy with). We talked about housing and about coping with the English weather. We reminisced about childhood memories.

Then all too soon I was homeward bound. The closer to Jan Smuts we got, the more palpable the anxiety attack. As the pilot announced touch-down, I was trembling.

What had I said? To whom? Who had asked me what and why? Of the numerous people I had met and talked to, who might be in the pay of the government? Belatedly, pitfalls became as obvious as a molehill on the wayside.

An elaborate system to verify my safe arrival had been set up after the conference. If so-and-so did not hear from so-and-so by such-and-such a time, she would contact another person to see what was going on. If something had happened to me or there was no trace of me, women in different countries would raise a cry.

All this might seem melodramatic to some, like a case of overreaction or hysteria or taking ourselves a little too seriously. But that I did not enjoy protection from the law had shaken many a delegate. That the law was in fact designed for my oppression had staggered more.

By the time I got off the plane at Jan Smuts Airport I had shed quite a bit of my carry-on luggage. Any book or magazine whose purity I was not a hundred per cent sure of, I abandoned right there on that plane. I was not about to invite hostile questions from customs officials who would like to use me as a lesson to other uppity kaffirs who went to places they had no business going to.

Mindful of the fact that I annoyed these people by my mere existence, my ability to go overseas a sore point to them, why would I want to irritate them further by bringing into the country literature they did not recognise from their Standard Six reading list? Remember, the book *Black Beauty* was once banned in South Africa.

I reached my family without a hitch. At my job I was given a party fit for a celebrity.

Predictably, a member of the Special Branch paid me a visit. Where had I gone? Why? Whom had I met? Why? Who was —? Where did I know them from? The solidarity I had felt at the conference gave me some solace, some hope that I wouldn't be forgotten should the authorities decide to arrest me.

Many are the women I met at this conference: all warm and accepting. They wished me well. They wished me courage. We exchanged addresses. We wanted to keep in touch. And some did write to me. I may have answered one or three. But the fear that enveloped me on my return to South Africa and especially after yet another visit from the Special Branch made me reluctant to display symptoms of being 'tainted'. I craved the obscurity that would make the authorities forget about me. I was absolutely shocked at how I'd become known, noticed by them ... having done nothing at all, in my opinion, to warrant such attention.

Thus rejuvenated, I immersed myself in work and studies.

I had been back in the country but two months when the monster hatched.

Twelve

On 16 June 1976 Soweto burst into flame. I had been back from the Brussels Conference for two months. What had started as a students' boycott of classes was mishandled by the government and escalated into an insurrection that would be remembered for years to come. Decades. African students were demanding reform in the education system.

We watched in horror as violence spread. Reports of police brutality were in every news bulletin. But that was up north, far away from me. My immediate world was intact. Or so it seemed to me.

Soon, however, the riots that had broken out in Soweto spread to other centres of the country, urban and rural, big and small. They were unpredictable, spontaneous and surprising in their intensity and the intense response they provoked.

The riots were long overdue. Like death, the events of 1976 had not hurried, they had bided their time, certain of their mark and sure of their potency.

1976 was born of events near and far, in terms of both time and geography. With the independence of Ghana, some twenty years before, the seed of freedom had sprouted in the heart of the black man in South Africa and grown roots that would never shrivel again. In direct proportion to the growing restlessness within the black man, the white man dug in his heels, promulgated even more vicious and repressive laws, and deepened his faith that he would continue to lord it over the black man till the end of time.

Like chickens in the calm before a whirlwind, South

Africans had worn disquiet for long, weary years. Cooped up in our pen, we fluttered, beat and bruised our wings; we sent out loud cries both shrill and low; we pecked at each other's eyes, scratched and drew blood with our talons. But the mesh, three strands strong, held us in check. With everything pure in us warning us of the impending hurricane that would sweep us all away, we could not save ourselves.

Now, hundreds of kilometres away from where I sat, safe in the knowledge of that vast shielding distance, African children, school children, left their classes and took to the streets. Aloud, aggressively but peacefully, they voiced their grievances.

Their grievances were those of all Africans, young and old, parent and child. Nothing the student said then or after was new. It had been said all along that the education of the African child was appallingly inferior to that of the white child. Any fool could figure that out. Not much could be bought for twenty-eight rand a year – the amount the government gave for the education of an African child. The same government had no qualms in lavishing four hundred and eighty rand each year on the education of one white child. Since its inception, Bantu Education had been condemned by its consumers, the Africans. Without exception, teachers and parents said it was not only not good enough, it was poison.

I have experienced Bantu Education – as a student, as a teacher, as a parent; and I would not hesitate to advocate its total eradication. Nothing in it merited the name of education.

And that is what the students were objecting to. They were categorically rejecting this thing that was paraded as education, when it had long been apparent that it was the farthest thing from an education and known to all as inferior, degrading, unworthy of the designation.

Bantu Education had long been resented. But it took a government initiative to spark off the protests. Afrikaans, the second official language of South Africa, had become the third language African students had to learn. A decade after its introduction into our schools, the government decided our children were not learning it fast enough, and to remedy that it decreed that Afrikaans be used as a medium of instruction for fifty percent of the school subjects. Even for people as obtuse as the policy-makers in South Africa, this step was sheer folly. How did they justify forcing pupils and students to be taught through a language they did not understand? Moreover, was this not a complete reversal of an earlier stipulation, that of mother tongue instruction?

To say this was the last straw that broke the camel's back would be an error. This was no straw but a whole bundle of thick heavy logs. Afrikaans, rightly or not, was closely associated with the government and its abhorred system of apartheid. It had been hardship enough to learn the language, but to be asked to learn through it removed the last veneer of decency in Bantu Education and laid naked its agenda: the stunting of the African child.

The students took to the streets, declaring the system of education designed exclusively for them as 'poison' that had to 'be abolished'.

The protests, fuelled by the government, turned into riots. But at first the riots were confined to the Witwatersrand. As news from the battle-front filtered through to my part of the country, I held my breath in fear: the fear of those who smell not the acrid smoke of gunpowder or the fumes from burning flesh. The fear of fear.

Then one day, while I was busy teaching – was it a Xhosa poem or the copulative formed from a noun? – bands of students marched right up to the fence of St Gabriel's Catholic Church at N.Y. 5.

A delegation of two or three students detached itself from that living, heaving multitude and came inside the church yard. Two of our student leaders, Temba Matomela and the late Godfrey Ndungane, went to meet them. They returned to tell us teachers that the students wanted us to close shop and demanded that our students join in the protest. In one short day, the protests had come to Cape Town.

At the sight of that throng, I knew my world would never be the same again. What I did not know was the nature and the magnitude of that change. A decade and a half later, I still have but an inkling of what the events of 1976 signified. Sadly, I am not alone in this limited vision. And the aftermath of the storm unfolds still.

16 August: Langa, Guguletu and Nyanga exploded. The riots had come to Cape Town.

When the students marched to Inxaxheba, the study centre run from St Gabriel's, and demanded that our students join them, Sr Aine, who ran the centre, was abroad, if I'm not mistaken. I was the most senior teacher at the time and was, with the help of another colleague, overseeing the project. Our two young men returned. '*Sis'* Sindi,' they said, for that is how everyone addressed me at the centre, 'those students say we must join them. They say we should not be in school.'

We were not a school. Our students were young people who, for a variety of reasons, had already left the formal school sector. Yes, they were preparing for the same examinations, but this was not a BAD [Bantu Affairs Department] school. It wasn't a school at all. We ran tutorials for the students. They wore no uniform. They were more active participants in their education than they would ever have been in a formal school environment. They addressed us as we were addressed in the township: *Sis'* or *Bhut'* – and not Ma'm, Miss, Sir or Teacher. Moreover, we, the tutors, were not in the payroll of the Department of Bantu Education, and I was in fact the only tutor with any teacher training.

But in face of the demands made to us that day – 'We don't want to have to come into the church premises and force you out!' – and after hasty consultations among us all, teachers and students, the decision was made to let the students leave the premises.

We gathered in the hall, and I asked the students to stand in a circle. Tutors joined in. We held hands. My eyes were filled with tears as I looked at those young faces – young men and women – and wondered what would happen to them. Would they ever regain the opportunity to resume their studies? An opportunity that was already, for all of them, a second chance? Remember, these were students who had already been thrown out by the system. A few were older than the average student. Most had problems at home, and Inxaxheba was their last hope, their only hope of gaining a matric and, with it, some slight promise of employment or opportunity for further studies.

We stood in a circle and I said a short prayer. I had never felt more inadequate in my life. What was my prayer in the face of the force blowing through the land? Perhaps I am a person of little faith. But I understood the desperate anger and frustration that had sired the eruption. I had gone around warning of exactly this kind of disaster. And now it had come, and I was not ready for its fury.

My world that had seemed so safe only yesterday became the scene of marching students, attacking police, running students, bewildered parents. Burning buildings, looting, killing and worse abominations played before our eyes during those tortured days. The sky turned the bleached blue of a pigeon's egg and our lives took the brittle texture of its shell.

People who had done so much to avert just this, now showed their mettle.

CWC women galvanised themselves into a mini United Nations task force during the students' riots in Guguletu, Langa and Nyanga. The authorities had sealed off the African townships, and no deliveries could be made to them. Soon the townships ran dry. No paraffin could be found in the local shops. Without paraffin, no one in Guguletu could cook, as the township was innocent of electricity. Bread, milk and other essentials could not be bought anywhere in Lagunya, the composite township of Langa, Guguletu and Nyanga.

CWC members who lived outside Lagunya organised supplies: paraffin, milk, bread, meat, tea, coffee, beans, sugar, candles, samp, vegetables, medical supplies and more. They gave their cars to be driven into the townships by black men whom they did not know. Whites, always forbidden to enter African residential areas unless they had been given a permit, were not about to be allowed into these areas now they were on fire.

These women, divided into white and coloured by most, but known to me and others like me as ordinary human beings, women full of compassion, took into their homes children, the sick and the elderly – people fleeing consuming, blind terror that threatened them with obliteration.

The riots took everybody by surprise. The parents of the rioting students were taken by surprise. Their children had chosen to go it alone, accusing them of acquiescence. The government was taken by surprise. That was by student design. The students were taken by surprise. They had expected the inevitable reaction from the government but what they had not dreamt of was the unleashing of the army on them.

Unarmed, they had not believed they posed enough of a threat to warrant such a counter-attack. A war in all but name ensued. Might pitted against right.

It was hell living in the townships then. It always had been terrible living in the townships. But now everything was highlighted and concentrated. An impatient, indiscriminate, red-hot ball of ire.

When no more government targets were available, the delivery vans that dared enter the townships were highjacked, off-loaded and set on fire. This on-the-spot redistribution of food was labelled *Umbumbumbu* in the African townships. *Umbumbumbu!* The cry would sound and people raced towards the source, to avail themselves of whatever was for the taking. The objectives had shifted:

'Apartheid cannot be reformed. It must be destroyed,' shouted the students, fervent in their undertaking.

'We are ready for anything. We shall quell this communist-inspired violence. We shall get the agitators,' replied the government, murderously serious.

Loud voices. Many voices. Agitated, excited voices. Voices that sounded like a flood, then like a migrating swarm of locusts. I look out of the window. The young people are all over the field opposite my house. Somewhere in the centre that keeps shifting, there is a bunching. Are those taller youngsters? No, they are on a van. They are in it. Around it. On it. One can't even see the colour it is. The van is in motion, slow motion.

The van humps to a halt. The 'driver' gets out. The van's load is tipped onto the ground and the young people flee. *Mbumbumbu! Mbumbumbu!* The cry fills the air.

Not all are students.

Are *those* students?

It became increasingly difficult to say. Students. Sympathisers. Scoundrels who, thrilling to the lawlessness, joined the struggle and plunged it into anarchy.

Others – men, women and young people who were not in the students' war, children too young to be in it – all these people descended like vultures and helped themselves to the spoils.

Each person takes as much as he or she can carry and runs. An hour later or sooner the police or the army or both will arrive on this scene, notified by the driver of the van. Woe to anyone found anywhere near the wreck.

On this day, after the van had been emptied of its contents, it was set alight. We watched from the relative safety of our houses, the more daring in their yards and the reckless on the street nearer the van, which is lying on its side and burning away.

It was late in the afternoon when a young man, a neighbour, happened on the scene on his way from work. When he came across the smouldering van and the refuse all around it, he stopped for a closer look. It still lay on its side, a thin curl of smoke lazily hovering above it. The van and its plight had long ceased to be of any interest to both the township Robin Hoods and the beneficiaries of their efforts. He took his time, trying to recreate in his mind the scene he had missed, just awed at the spectacle of the gutted van. The police found Vuyani thus occupied.

No one asked him why, what, when or how. He was beaten senseless.

He is one of the lucky ones who lived to tell the tale. Now he walks with a pronounced limp and his speech is a little slurred. And he still suffers from seizures and is a little diminished in capacity. Vuyani's story is but one of the numerous stories of those sad days. Tales of horror stunned and numbed us. Parents watched helpless as their children were shot right inside their homes.

On this day, the police fell upon Vuyani. He was kicked. Batons banged on his head, on his back, on any part they could find. In seconds he was down, bleeding from head wounds, bleeding through the nose, the mouth ... it was difficult to say where exactly. Blood spurted and spattered all over his body, onto the ground where he lay completely inert.

One family saw their two boys run inside, the police in hot pursuit. Home that day failed to be a haven. The boys, sensing the wrath of their chasers, ran straight through the house: in by the front door, out by the back and into the toilet where they closed the door.

The police were not deterred.

The father tried talking to the police, who made not a sign they had seen or heard him as they stomped determinedly through his house. The man watched his two sons hauled out and shot at point-blank range. Their hands up in the air. Their bare, bare hands.

A car with a mother carrying her sick child on her back was stopped by the police. She was on her way to the doctor. In the ensuing car search, a police bullet found its way into the baby's head. She died.

Despite claims and counter-claims of responsibility for what took place in the townships of South Africa in 1976, I doubt the students riots in 1976 were instigated by anything but the motivation of the students. Motivation rooted in frustration, in anger and in despair that things would ever get better. The government claimed the riots were communist-inspired, the work of agitators, and alluded to the organisations and people it had banned and forced out of the country. This was an insult to the students. It was saying they did not have the brains to see that they were getting a raw deal.

The students left the classrooms and congregated on school grounds where they held meetings. They left their own schools and went to meet with others at a central school. From school to school they walked. Thousands of African youth, in different school uniforms, marched with furious purpose written on their fired faces to a central point in Guguletu.

As long as they demonstrated their dissatisfaction, no blood was spilled. As long as the students did what they had planned to do, things were fine.

But the government was irritated by this condemnation. It was one thing that the Africans did not appreciate what the government was doing for them, but quite another when that ungratefulness was flaunted for the whole world to see.

The press first reported what was happening in the townships. And the government reacted to the reports of the press as well as to what was happening in the townships.

If the press made heroes of the students, the government

felt slighted and on the next day came with a show of strength. If the press made the government, police or soldiers look bad, government spokesmen issued denials, explanations and protestations of press bias.

Then the government barred the students from schools and school grounds.

Barred from school grounds, barred from holding their meetings, the students lashed out at the government. Only the government was far removed from the African townships. Yet it did have some presence there. Had it not built shadows of libraries, inadequate schools, makeshift post offices, well-stocked bottle-stores and solid-structured administration buildings there? On these brick representatives of the government, the students wreaked their vengeance.

Riots escalated, sweeping across the country like a veld fire. Some of the coloured schools caught a spark and burst into flame. Coloured students with better laboratory facilities than their African brethren knew how to make Molotov cocktails. No sooner had the coloured students joined the riots than these weapons rained on police vans, even in the African townships. Coloured and African students had learnt to share knowledge. How ironic that it could only be in this way. But who is to blame for that except the government and its policy of segregation?

Mesh guards were put on police-van windows. Now and then things would cool off in this or that black area. The media would announce that uncanny quiet reigned in the township. Quiet and the absence of riots belonged to white neighbourhoods. If riots happened in the townships, they were news. When nothing happened in black areas, the media made that news. Bold headlines.

That is how I learnt that no news could be a great deal of news, that the media not only reported news but made it too.

VAN OVERTURNED IN GUGULETU

CARS STONED ON WAY TO AIRPORT

ALL QUIET IN LANGA

It was a safe bet that Langa would not be quiet the next day.

It was a year of great learning in the townships. We learnt new smells, the sound of stuttering guns. We learnt faster ways of running. We learnt new meanings of fear, bolder loyalty, and ways of betrayal which we had never thought of before. Darker shades of despair came to visit, overstayed their welcome, and today like an amputated toe mark every step we take.

I never fully understood, never quite knew what was happening in our townships in 1976. I doubt many did, and in that many I include some of the players. Not that I was a complete bystander.

Not only had I predicted, in numerous speeches and presentations, the violence now sweeping through the townships of the Western Cape and the whole country, I had alerted others to its coming and urged them to prepare themselves for its fury.

If they were ready, good for them. I was completely unready and daily, in direct proportion to the growing conflagration, I saw myself go crazy. No one else seemed to notice my altered state. Or if they did, they certainly did not let on.

At the beginning, there was order. The civil disobedience was ordered. It had clear objectives, clear direction, and a clear voice.

Young school-going Africans had had enough of the education given them. Desirous of change, they decided to take to the streets, to let the government know that they were ready for change. I was wholly behind the students. I shared their sentiments about our education without reservation.

At first, the students did not ask for adult participation. They did not want it. They were working for themselves. But as the government responded in ways the students had not perhaps anticipated, the involvement of other people became not only necessary but crucial.

The students needed cars. They needed petrol. They needed money. They needed food. They needed medicine and sometimes doctors. And when they were jailed, their needs didn't stop. They needed visitors – people to keep watch. Things happened there. And a life could depend on whether there was anyone outside paying attention. They needed parents. They needed lawyers and advocates. They needed priests. And they needed their message to go on being heard.

Their numbers swelled. Their voice did change. Or perhaps it was the note that did. Whatever it was, something in what the students said they were doing altered.

Where we parents had previously looked on with grudging admiration, now we began to tremble with trepidation. Confusion spread, chasing the fear racing from heart to heart to heart. It caught up with the fear, fertilised it, and the fear swelled and swelled and, in due course, bore forth its bitter fruit.

I do not now recall exactly who it was that approached me to serve on Lagunya, a committee representative of Langa, Guguletu and Nyanga residents. How many of us were in that committee? I remember Father Matolengwe of Holy Cross, the Anglican church in Nyanga. Mrs Nomvula Mtetwa may have been on the committee, likewise the late Mr Phillips, a prominent businessman and Langa resident. I remember distinctly that Lagunya was kept deliberately small.

There may have been only six of us, two for each township. Community meetings were frequent. Lagunya's purpose was to manage the crisis, as far as that could be done. It also received and disbursed emergency funds.

I attended most of the community meetings, being as concerned as the next parent about the whole thing. I gave my opinion at these meetings, and gave it sincerely.

But parents were not the only non-students who were getting involved. The three children of fear and confusion –

Cowardice, Corruption and Colonisation – had arrived.

Suddenly I did not know what I knew or who I knew. With the exception of my mother, my own sisters and brothers, and my own children, I did not know anyone at this time.

Some neighbours sprouted horns that could gore me. Colleagues I had known and trusted grew tails. And friends had the Devil's own fire roaring, ready to fry me to brittle bone.

The pressure was fierce for people, everybody, to be involved in what was happening. But not all did so out of conviction.

Cowardice, the firstborn child, ruled many. At meetings, raised voices supported the insupportable. Absorbed in my little world of order and meaning, a world of purpose and a tomorrow, I lost popularity with brutal swiftness, like losing virginity to a rapist.

Once, after a meeting which left me much bewildered, I enquired of a friend who'd been an adversary during the meeting: 'Tell me,' I said, 'what is it I am missing? I don't understand how you can go along with what was proposed in there.'

Came the response, sophisticated, calculated and hot in its coldness:

'I am not going to have my house burnt down by the comrades.'

Dear God! How depressed such answers made me feel. How depressed and how anguished. For I also knew that not one thought of betrayal lay in the hearts of people like that. People like that would rather have died than sabotage the struggle of the students.

If the students had planned the boycotting of classes, they had not planned the participation of their parents in the struggle. Now, some (if not most) of the adults participating did so because they were coerced, forced, or shamed into it. Their involvement did not arise from desire, never mind conviction.

A lot of the coercion had come with the colonisation of the leadership of the boycotts. As the authentic student leaders were arrested, jailed, killed, forced to go underground or fled the country, others were quick to fill their shoes. Unfortunately, not all were qualified to lead. And not a few were not even students.

Now came corruption. The means became the consuming end. The bandwagon threatened to keel over, so overladen it was. Jack, Jill and Trollop had got on, bringing their families, their friends and their foes along for the ride.

I wonder how many of the zealots of this hour drink liquor today. Let us remember, these are the same young people who pushed their fingers down the throats of their fathers and forced them to bring up the liquor they had drunk. Tell me, please tell me, that today the liquor trade is near collapse, deprived of African consumers of a certain age.

You went along or you shut your mouth and prayed your eyes did not give you away. You did not disagree openly. Fools who did were labelled informers. 'You are either part of the solution or you're part of the problem' – a slogan from yesterday had taken on a new face, a sterner face. A face that could kill.

I became part of the problem. Madness completely engulfed me. Sane people made certain that they made no choices. Sane people who understood what was happening took a stand. They 'ayed' whatever the comrades said. Some of the 'comrades' didn't even know how to write that word; students they certainly were not. Reformers! Don't make me cry for my beloved people.

Being born under a stubborn sign, a blind sign of meticulous ways, I could not see that the time had come for me to kill my personal standards. I have never been much good at the art of camouflaging my feelings. I have not yet to this day learnt how to play games with words I do not mean.

What if I had raised children who had set times for coming home in the evening? There was a struggle on. The call was out for young people – boys and girls – to be abroad at late hours of the night, I was told.

'My children will not set foot out of this house at night.' I stood my ground. Jesus! They were my children. I had raised them. Alone. I had had to be more father than mother to them, fearing the looseness that I heard characterises homes headed by females. Children brought up by *idikazi* were not expected to amount to much. I had been bringing mine up to amount to more than much, painfully aware of the burden they already carried. Even as I made an all-out effort to give my children some semblance of order in their lives, I feared the absence of a male head of the family would thwart my well-laid plans.

From the time, a decade before, that I'd found myself solely responsible for my children, I'd been on a crusade. My children were going to amount to something; they would amount to something and to much more than most children from intact families. And I drilled that truth into their heads early in their lives.

'Listen to me and open your ears wide. Make sure you clear your ears of all wax. You have no father. You are being raised by *idikazi*. People expect you to be nothing. They are waiting for you to turn rotten. Now, you make sure you don't help them in that opinion of you.' I would lecture them long on how if one of their friends who had a mother and a father did something wrong in the eyes of the community, that would be a mistake on the child's part. The parents would receive commiseration from the community: 'Aren't today's children something?' 'After all you are doing for her, how could she do this?'

But if the same things were done by one of them, I warned my children, the whole world would nod its sad head and say, 'Ah! But what did you expect? The child is being raised by a woman of questionable character, after all.'

And today I was being told my children should listen to the commands of other children. Should go to meetings at night.

The commands came with threats. 'They will come and get those children who do not attend the meetings.'

At that point I decided I would die parenting my children. No child of mine – they were then thirteen, eleven and ten – would go about unchaperoned at night. And I was prepared and let it be known I was prepared for the students to come to my door. I had my armour: the truth. If these students were honest, I was safe, I fiercely wanted to believe.

So, believing in my truth, believing in that truth as my salvation against the threat of sanctions from the 'comrades', I put my foot down. Fortunately for me, how firmly it was put down was never put to the test. But I earned the scorn of a great number of people who saw my stand as counter-revolutionary. I lost a lot of respect, a lot more credibility. But friends stood by me.

The centre shifted during that dividing year. I stopped knowing what was happening, what was about to happen, or why it was happening. My prophesies had turned out to be a reality uglier than any nightmare I could have had.

The blind fury of which I had warned had come. Wave upon wave, gathering and sweeping indiscriminately all in their wake, and gathering strength as they went on and on and on. Relentless.

I had seen it coming, and yet when it came, I didn't know it. When it came, it did not have one face, it did not have one mind and it certainly did not speak one language. Indeed, it spoke no known language at all.

Scarred, scared and scantily clad with wisdom, I reluctantly looked at myself in the mirror and what I saw frightened me even more. Where was I? Who was I? For the mirror showed me someone I was not, someone I remembered as from a past long ago.

The fury shrunk me.

Everyone was caught up in it. There was no escape from it. The rich, the old, the young, the frail, the poor, the learned, and the unschooled – all were in one place. One big place. Everyone agreed it had had to come. No one knew why they, as ordinary as they were, could not be left alone to limp along the best way they knew, as they had been doing for so long.

Looking back now, I find it hard to believe so much could have happened in such a short time. An uneasy calm settled on Cape Town as the year limped to a gasping end. Never again would I wonder how 'May you live in exciting times' could be a curse.

A good deal had been lost, some said. A good deal had been won, said others. Which is true? All I know is that we were all changed by that sieving year.

Thirteen

The bloodshed tugged at the hearts of the women of Cape Town. They called a meeting of women of all colours, languages and races, irrespective of class. The City Hall opened its doors wide, and thousands of women flocked there on the appointed day like lost souls seeking refuge.

Twelve speakers shared the platform. I was one of them.

We spoke of the pain our eyes had been forced to see. The death of young and old had brought us there. We examined the reasons for the boycotts, and we spoke long and clear of the hard life of the township dwellers, a life definitely without relief.

The anger, bred of the violence that had brought us there, was thick. Views, testimony and opinion flowed freely.

That meeting was the birth of the Women's Movement. At the end of the speeches, the women resolved that a movement be started there and then.

A movement of women – the mothers, wives, sisters, lovers and friends of the white boys whom the government was turning each year into canon-fodder in an unjust war on South Africa's borders. A movement of the women who together with their men and their children had been denuded of the very foundation of a meaningful life – disenfranchised, disowned, oppressed and relegated to the status of perpetual servitude.

Forced estrangement of the people of the land was blamed. Our young were growing up complete strangers, though they were compatriots. The root of all the rot, agreed the women, was how we were arranged as a society. It thus became clear to those assembled there that day what the remedy would be.

These women said they would fight the menace that split them as women, that split families and the very soul of each one of them. By the end of the meeting, the women of Cape Town had formed themselves into an organisation: the Women's Movement. The word 'peace' was deliberately omitted. There was a feeling it might cloud the organisation's objective, people might get confused or misinterpret what the organisation stood for – solving the problems that antedated the tumult – not the static peace we had 'enjoyed' prior to the riots: an absence of overt opposition to oppression.

I joined the Women's Movement the day it was formed and sat on its Executive Committee until late 1978 when I bowed out of all bridge-building and all attempts at working for peaceful change in South Africa.

We held meetings. We gave talks. We wrote letters to the press. We protested against segregation in schools, restaurants and public transport. We defied tradition and arranged group activities, making sure these groups were representative of the full spectrum of South Africa's people. We approached government officials with our insights. We went from door to unyielding door with petitions.

I was so busy that my family hardly saw me. I would leave home at the crack of dawn for work and return only in the wee hours of the morning, having put in a meeting or two after work. It was not unheard of that I would address a meeting during lunch hour. My world had turned upside down, inside out, and the idea of righting it became a personal crusade. I wanted my children and their children after them to have a home in this country, a happy home, safe and nurturing.

As education came to a bloody stop for Africans (and later for coloured students), my energies went more and more into working for peaceful change. What had absorbed me, now devoured me. I had to cling to something for the centre had shifted.

I was one of the speakers at a seminar on 'The Migratory Labour System' given at the University of Cape Town. There I met a man who was working for a conglomerate of farms, Groot Drakenstein Fruit Farms.

Rolf Hartig had been sitting in the audience. Midway through my speech, this man began mopping his eyes. During question time, he asked me whether I would help him convince his bosses of the need to change the housing of their farm labourers.

By the end of 1977, those twenty farms, collectively known as Groot Drakenstein Fruit Farms, had built a model village with modern conveniences for their migrant workers. The workers themselves had had much input in the project, especially as regards standards and maintenance. There were even special quarters for the occasions when some of the wives or families might come to visit. Not an ideal solution to be sure. But for those men this was an improvement of great magnitude from the squalid hovels in which they had been living, an improvement all welcomed and few had ever hoped to witness.

Rolf Hastig's response and what it led to are an example of the kind of small miracle that spurred me and others on. There were, however, some whose response dampened our spirits and left us feeling like inflatable dolls who had been punctured by some unruly boy.

It is not easy, when one has just spilled one's bleeding guts out, baring one's soul, one's pain, to complete strangers, hoping to save them and hoping thus to save oneself, to be confronted with questions like these:

'What can we do for you people?'

'What do your people want?'

'You have to understand something. Poverty exists in other countries too. I have just come back from Italy. The poverty in Italy is appalling! I saw people walking barefoot there. And these were *white* people.' And the speaker looks to me for sympathy, for understanding.

'Oh, where did you learn your English?' A comment that spoke volumes about the white view that we would never become educated despite our going to school.

'Nobody gave us what we have. We worked for it.' Why do white people think black people play at work? Who doesn't work? Do white people not see the waiters, the cooks, the dish-washers, the nannies, the gardeners, the street sweepers, the chauffeurs, the farm and mine workers, the milkmen, the delivery men, the smiling doormen and the overalled cleaners of home and office? Do they not see the men and women who fill their cars with petrol at the filling stations?

'Why do you people have so many children?' This one floors me. I know destitute childless people.

'You complain about conditions here. I wish you could go to those independent countries in Africa. You would see how lucky you are.'

'You people are impatient. The government is making changes.' This is older than the hills.

'Why don't you go to your own countries?' And I think, she probably came here ten years ago from England or elsewhere in the British Isles, she or her mother before her. Now she points to a barren tract of land she has never seen and calls it 'your country'. The homelands resolved a lot of guilt for those whites with any guilt left.

'We white people have a higher standard of living to maintain. That is why we get higher salaries. Do you know how much rent I have to pay?'

Fact. These people, I told myself, didn't have to be at the meeting. Their very presence indicates, if not eagerness to change the *status quo*, at least a dim awareness of that fact.

To those who showed ignorance about our needs, to those who would enlighten us about our enormous good fortune of being black and poor in South Africa and not white and poor in Italy or some similarly afflicted country, and to the goodhearted who simply wished us away to 'another' country that was our very own, to all these concerned South African whites of goodwill, the simple truth was lost: we are people too. We are South Africans too. We, too, want our due.

And as if this spurious verbiage was not enough to drive a person to murderous thoughts, similar thoughts would sometimes come from the white women with whom we were busy working for peaceful change. For me, that was the worst, the most hurtful, being the least expected.

Lulled into a false sense of safety, believing that these *verligte* whites understood my humanity and accepted our being of the same species, I would be stabbed by:

'But, Sindi, how representative are you of the black people?'

Discussing sanctions in 1977, I found myself being accused by a white woman of elitism. The Women's Movement was groping for a stand on this issue. We had met on that particular afternoon to formulate strategy. In the course of discussing the pros and cons of sanctions, which I happened to support at that time, my colleague shot out:

'But it will hurt black people more.'

I painstakingly explained that black people had been suffering all along. Their infants were dying. Their children suffered from malnutrition and died of measles. Their children were killed in thousands each year, by diseases such as diphtheria, whooping cough, tetanus, poliomyelitis and tuberculosis, diseases that, were white South Africa so to desire, could be prevented from killing black children, in the same way they had been stopped from killing white children. But my explanations went unheeded.

My appeal that international intervention was the only solution left, internal solutions having failed, fell on deaf ears.

'Sindi, *you* are educated. *You* are sophisticated. How do you know what black people, the ordinary black person in the street, want? My mouth flew open – but not a sound came out. An inflated frog blocked my throat. I swallowed hard, but nothing went down. There was nothing in my mouth … in my throat. All dryness. All feeling had fled.

What hit me was the irony of such an attack by a white woman who, seeing me as not black, forgot that somewhere in the not too distant past I must have been uneducated and poor. That was more than she could claim.

If I was taking such abuse from whites who were progressive enough to work with black people, I was facing worse from the township, my home.

'She is an informer.'

'Why is she always with whites?'

'How do you think she gets all those good jobs?'

'I saw her in Claremont in a car with two white women.'

'I saw her in Observatory in a car parked in a little dark street with a white man.'

'Her children and her younger siblings visit white homes to play with white children.'

'How do you think she has stayed out of jail when she goes around the country talking bad about the government?'

'That one is an informer. Everybody knows that.' This was the unkindest cut of all. But since nobody had come to make the accusation to my face, I chose to ignore it. The few friends with whom I brought it up either took it lightly – 'Ooh, Sindi, you know that is not so!' as if *my* opinion was what mattered – or simply reassured me: 'But you know who started that rumour and why she started it.'

I did know. For a few years after my husband left me I did not hate men; in fact my best friends were men. But I shunned intimate involvement with a man. Then a friend took pity on me and introduced me to her boyfriend's cousin. I took to him like a duck to water. While it lasted, it was good. But he was Catholic and when time came for him to marry, well, not only was I out of the running because I'd been married before, but I wasn't even divorced. Then followed other affairs, nothing serious, nothing I couldn't handle. And then there came Bunny.

For four full years we were so happy I forgot the meaning of misery. I was so secure in this relationship that I blossomed. I had never, even as a younger woman, felt so loved. Bunny was tender and lavished me with attention. He was seven years younger and didn't care a stick about it. Friends from both sides of the alliance tried at first to warn us that it was infatuation. We paid them no heed. Four years. And then a childhood sweetheart of his came back to Cape Town.

I heard about her arrival from Bunny himself. He was good that way; no surprises. If he did anything he knew I would hate hearing, he would tell me himself and beat my friends and family members to it. By the time anyone came to me with a tale, I already knew. And so I went on feeling safe and loved.

We discussed the meaning of the return of the former lover. He had a choice to make. I made him see there was no way he could even think of having both of us. I was having none of that nonsense. Well, he decided to break with the other woman, who was younger than him and very pretty indeed. How happy I was! I did love him, and it would have been very hard for me to give him up or see him walk away.

A year or so later, I learnt that the two were seeing each other secretly. Bunny told me. And this time I took the decision that he should leave me alone. We parted company and, in due course, the couple had a child and moved in together.

The baby was hardly six months when they had a very serious fight involving disclosures which Bunny felt should have been made by the lady and had not been made. He felt he had been taken for a ride and was the laughing stock of the whole of Guguletu. As they were not married, saying goodbye was a matter of walking out of the door of the back room they sub-let from another family. Of course, as always with cases like this, there was the matter of the child. That linked them and made contact between them unavoidable.

It didn't take long after this for Bunny and me to be together once more. As I saw it, he was available now that he and the other woman had split. She, however, did not see it that way at all. She was incensed that he had come back to me, and treated the whole thing as if she had been betrayed or as if Bunny had chosen me over her.

There were scenes. There were threats. And in cowardice I refused to be drawn into a fight with this woman. Instead I told the man, the bone of contention, 'Please, sort out your business so that I am left alone.' And always, after I'd been upset by this woman and he'd had a word with her, I would be left alone for a while.

With the confusion caused by the turmoil of the late seventies, my personal life, always a little turbulent, took a plunge. I came to see a new face of anger, a new strength of venom, a fury I still find difficult to understand.

This woman, younger and truly beautiful, couldn't accept what she perceived as being outdistanced in the race for Bunny's heart. Fangs bared, she struck. She spread the rumour that I was an informer. To this day, although Bunny and I have long gone our separate ways, although I've put great distance between the me of that time and the me of today, the poison is in me. I walk with it, sleep with it, go to work with it. It knows everybody I know. Try shaking it away as I do, it follows me everywhere, poisoning all I encounter and experience.

My name, my good name, died in this attack. I lost my sense of trust, the trust I had that others take me at face value. The trust that truth always wins in the end.

What was hard to bear was the knowledge that I had all

the characteristics of an informer: my self-reliance, my refusal always to swim with the tide, forever questioning things others accepted even when they did not understand them, my exceeding individualism, my association with people I refused to classify according to the colour of their skin, seeing friends, human beings, where others saw colour and nothing but colour. My big mouth had finally landed me in an ocean of soup. And I, unable to swim even in clear water, nearly went under. I flapped around, all over the place.

After a while, I simply stopped talking about it, knowing a special private hell: how ready I had been to believe the same thing about someone else I knew. Scapegoating, the power of rumour, mud-slinging – I saw myself in all of these. And I tried very hard to understand how I was not the only victim. How even those who spread such evil about me were also victims. How it was a case of displaced aggression. I failed, miserably. I was far from consoled: I was scared. People killed informers with the ease and disregard of wringing a chicken's neck. And this was before the horror of necklacing.

I betook myself to the chapel of self-righteousness and self-centredness.

If they need that desperately to judge, condemn and hang, all without due process, it is because they know no better, I told myself. Knowing I had never hurt another by design, I trusted that the truth would set me free, one day. It's been a long wait.

White women had the option of fleeing once the going got too rough. Some had dual citizenship whereas I had difficulty trying to get South African citizenship. Late in 1976 South Africa granted 'independence' to the Transkei, and that event rendered me a non-citizen in the land of my birth. The white women, on the other hand, could pack up and go overseas or to other places within the country – whilst the law of the land tied me, like the serf of centuries gone, to the townships of the Western Cape. That is where my pass allowed me to live. That is where it allowed me to work.

It is not easy to change horses in mid-stream. I forged on, if with less certain steps. I was still a member of CWC, the Women's Movement and the National Council of African Women, and belonged to various other informal groups. I was studying through UNISA and was also a SACHED student. I tutored for SACHED, and taught Xhosa to small groups of whites, often at the home of one of the group.

It was about this time that a former colleague who still worked for Bantu Administration informed me that my file was in the strongroom.

To say this piece of intelligence frightened me would be putting it mildly. I was bordering on a breakdown. If someone had put me in cold storage for a year, I couldn't have gone colder.

Fear is cold. Cold and clammy. It gets right inside one's bones. It freezes the marrow and slowly oozes through the pores to lie in a thin crust on the skin. Fear. It makes you cold, inside and out.

I hadn't done anything criminal. That gave me no solace at all: 'Knowledge of one's innocence is no guarantee or insurance against arrest in South Africa.'

Yes, I remembered those words. We had said them often at SACHED. Said them in jesty seriousness. Now they mocked me with their deadly earnestness.

We had joked then, laughing because even the idea of my being arrested was absurd. I have never belonged to any organisation even pretending to be underground. I know my limitations too well. Moreover, I am the one who had hardly any carefree, young adulthood: I was middle-aged by twenty-three. So I never did get the opportunity of becoming a young fervent revolutionary. By the time I was talking change, it was with tones tempered with caution.

Fourteen

1977 slithered in like the giant snakes of my childhood folk-tales told round cosy fires in long-ago Gungululu, the village where I was born. There had been no observance of Christmas in the year just past. These were times when we made holy days instead of celebrating them. The order of things, cause and effect, the relationships I had learnt while growing up, had gone haywire. I would not have been the least surprised to hear that the ancestors had gone mad and were paying homage to humans. Life had turned upside down, inside out.

January's air hung heavy, hot and joyless. It made me dread the remaining eleven months. I wished I could hold time still. Uncomfortable though today was, it was the morrow's uncertainties that made me cower.

The whole country was an ogre that had swallowed too much, even for an ogre. Now it writhed and groaned, not knowing how to put out the fire burning deep inside its cavernous body.

However, in the midst of all this, crude basic needs demanded attention, refused to be deferred or to give deferment to matters of national importance. I had to get a job. African schools were an on-again, off-again affair. Clearly Inxaxheba was not about to re-open. And unlike Bantu Education teachers, we were not paid unless there were classes. For some time now, I had been making do with an assortment of odd jobs, nothing long term.

By this time, Mrs Nomvula 'Ray' Mtetwa, my friend and mentor, had also left Bantu Administration's employ. She was working for a religious group, Toc H, in an office on the Main Road in Claremont.

She picked me up one Monday morning early in January and we drove to Claremont to clean her office. We were doing just that when she called out:

'Look, *Sithandwa*, there's an ad here for a Xhosa teacher! Here's the phone. It's working. Go ahead, call!' I paused long enough to read the advertisement. Earlier that same morning, Nomalanga, one of my sisters, had shown me the same advertisement. I had not bothered explaining the reasons stacked against my getting that post. I knew she wouldn't understand. My younger siblings think the world of me: to them, it is inconceivable that anyone should turn their brilliant 'Sis' down. I knew better.

I looked at the advertisement again: Herschel. That is a private school. A very posh private school.

'*Sis*' Ray, you know ... they're probably looking for a white teacher. They....'

'Call them anyway,' replied my friend, adding, 'Don't make it easy for them.'

Even as I picked up the phone I was thinking: What is the matter with me? What do I think I'm doing? But *Sis*' Ray was looking; there was no shying away from calling Herschel. So I picked up the receiver and dialled.

'I am interested in the post advertised in this morning's paper.'

'The Xhosa teacher?'

'Yes, the Xhosa teacher.'

'Can you tell me a little about yourself?'

'Well, I'm a qualified teacher. I've just finished my B.A. at UNISA. I'll be graduating in May. I have taught at both the primary and high school level. I love Xhosa. And, by the way, I am Xhosa-speaking.'

This last was a signal. It would be a good start if we both knew I was African, I felt.

'That's interesting,' came the reply. The speaker was far

from rattled.

That's all? my mind screamed at me. Before I answered it, the voice said:

'Where are you calling from?'

'Oh, I'm right here in Claremont,' not thinking.

'Then why don't you come over and see me?'

'Oh, I couldn't. I'm here helping a friend clean her office in preparation for her moving in.' In a panic, I added, 'I'm not dressed for an interview.'

'We'll certainly take that into account. Please do come.'

'Okay. What time would be convenient?'

'How about eleven o'clock?'

'Eleven o'clock is fine.'

Things were moving fast. Too fast for me. Turning to *Sis'* Ray, I stammered (a sign I'm very nervous):

'The pr-r-r-rprr-rincipal wants me to g-gg-go there in an hour's t-tt-time.'

Having discussed this unexpected development and agreeing that they really wanted a white teacher but were too suave to say so, we decided I should go anyway.

I was wearing a mistake, even for cleaning: a mini dress I had bought just about the time the mini was going out of fashion. I could not bring myself to throw it away; it was new. I couldn't wear it either. I looked awful in the mini, especially as no-one else went around any longer thus attired, looking like a half-plucked chicken. And, to top it, I had flip-flops (beach thongs). Yes, with my very obvious bunions staring. Anyway, at ten minutes to eleven, *Sis'* Ray drove me up the road and dropped me off at the school.

'You don't remember me, I'm sure. I remember you very well after the talk you gave here about a year ago!' said Dr Silberbauer, the principal, smiling as we shook hands in greeting.

I knew then I had lost the job. The talks I gave could be interpreted as highly political by some. Schools, I knew, were nests of conservatism.

Dr Silberbauer was so elegant and beautiful and gracious. I spent more than half an hour with her, over tea, and I forgot what I was wearing.

Since I knew I was not going to get the job anyway, I decided to be frank. I relaxed. The interview went very well. Imagine the jolt, therefore, when at the end of the interview she said:

'Well, I have to meet with the Board. They make the appointments, the actual hiring. But since they base that on my recommendation, I can tell you now, you've got the job.' People can kill you with shocks like that. I don't know if Dr S knew how close she came to dealing with a corpse. Sure, I'd have died happy from this unexpected news – but, dead is dead.

We shook hands, exchanged season's greetings and I left. As I walked towards the Main Road, I was not at all sure that I knew what had happened in that office. I could not believe I had been promised the job. I had studied long hours, part-time, by correspondence. Many in the township had openly laughed at me.

I had plodded on because the alternative was too horrendous to consider. Stagnation. End to expectation. No more dreams. I could not condemn myself to that. I had to have something to anticipate. And now, when jobs such as this one seemed to be thrust into my lap, I was surprised I could be singled out in that way.

And this was no empty promise either. I got the job. Herschel and I made a record of sorts: I had never before worked at the same job for more than two years. I was at Herschel for four full years.

I had definitely wandered beyond the boundaries of my prescribed life. My life was no longer confined to the African township, as the government wanted it to be. My limited horizon had widened. Among close friends, I counted people not classified Bantu. I visited them at their homes, and they came to mine and met my family just as I met theirs. As a result of the talks I gave I sometimes got invited to dinners at foreign embassies. I dined at restaurants which I hadn't even dared approach for a job – not as a waitress but as a scullery girl or cleaner.

Later that same year, I was among ten finalists for the *Cape Argus* Woman of the Year Award. I lived Social Responsibility. Not that I saw myself as a great martyr. My life just seemed to expand in new directions all the time. Hardly something to complain about.

I wore my newfound commitment like a halo; it went with me everywhere I went. It walked the streets with me, to and from work, shop, church or meeting.

Many shops in the Cape Peninsula have a practice of physically dragging prospective customers inside. Salesmen and saleswomen entice the passersby with 'Come inside and see', or similar words designed to lure you inside where you'll be softened into a purchase you had not intended.

One man who worked in one of the shops on Station Road, Claremont, was thoroughly offensive. *'MaDlamini! MaDlamini!'* he'd yell whenever an African woman happened to be passing by. Now I have nothing against the Dlamini clan. However, to lump together all African women is just not right. Like calling all Irish women Mrs Murphy … it is racist.

Trust me to take it up with this man. Hey, this was the new me, brand new and afire. I had seen the light. Why would I spare others the good tidings?

'Why do you call us all *MaDlamini?*' I asked him one day.

His answer was a question. 'What do you want me to call you?'

'What do you call other women passing here who are not African?' To which he wanted to know why I was making a fuss since the other women did not mind.

'You mean *African* women? You only say *MaDlamini* to African women, you know.'

We wrangled and argued, our voices going steadily higher. I accused him of racism, 'This is another way of saying Kaffir.' To which he shot back, 'Go away! You just showing off that you *ejucated.*'

SACHED had enabled me to get a UNISA degree. I still tutored for SACHED. My involvement with both the Women's Movement and Church Women Concerned was at its height. And this does not begin to paint a clear picture of the things I was up to. Mothering, neighbouring, going to church and to National Council of African Women meetings, and helping students, young and old, to pass examinations – Junior Certificate, matric, or UNISA.

At Herschel, I had a decent job. For once in the sixteen years since I had entered the world of work, the colour of my skin had nothing to do with the rand amount I took home on pay day. It was certainly far from a lean year for me.

Not that I was in danger of getting drunk from such success. Reality out there was ready to tailor me to pint size. On the day of the reception in honour of the finalists for the *Cape Argus* Award, I was on my way to a friend's house in Rondebosch. I was going there for a bath since Guguletu houses have no such facilities.

As I walked from the train station, the van parked on the side of the road told me I was in bad trouble. I had packed a change of clothing, beauty aids and other sundries I would probably need. Was my pass among the articles I had bothered to pack?

The Bantu Inspector (white, always white) watched me approach: 'Pass!'

Emboldened by encounters I had been having recently, I replied that I didn't have it on me but I could give him the identity number. After working for the Welfare Office for two years, the seven digits were as familiar to me as my surname: V/F 3472983-1. I rattled it off. Trust me to be a show-off, my life in danger. Relief! (I doubt it was admiration.) He then relayed the number to the driver. The latter used the walkie-talkie with which the van was equipped to contact the Administration Office in Langa. He must have found a little more than confirmation of my legal status in the prescribed area of the Cape Peninsula.

'You going to a meeting?' he asked, getting back into the van.

I replied I was visiting a friend, picked up my bag and walked off. Visiting a friend – for a black woman to have a friend in the white area was out of the usual. Of course, I could have been visiting a friend who was a live-in maid. Given my attire and the time of day – maids who work are not going to be entertaining friends at their places of work at five-ish in the afternoon – visiting a friend was therefore a bit cheeky, a verbal sticking-out of the tongue.

But 'meeting' – that bordered on the dangerous. People who go to meetings think, the government reckoned. A black woman who thought was a black woman who had forgotten her place.

In June 1978, I went to the USA as a participant in the International Visitors Programme. Six weeks to visit the country, meet people or groups of interest to me, see the sights I wanted to see. One does not apply but has to be nominated for this programme. My ancestors were surely doing their job.

The unstated aim of such trips is to expose those identified as leaders within their communities to the great democratic experience, the United States of America. This, so goes the thinking, will inculcate in the participants an undying admiration for the virtues of democracy.

This second overseas trip, more so than the first to Brussels two and a half years previously, had a tremendous impact on the direction my life would take henceforth.

A miracle. A once-in-a-lifetime experience. That had been my feeling about the Brussels trip. This second trip made me greedy. Surely if it can happen twice, it can happen three times, I reasoned.

On the return flight, I was already charting a strategy for my next trip. I wasn't fussy either about the country I would go to. The primary object was getting out of South Africa. How I would have leapt at a job as *au pair* or housemaid in a foreign land or with an emigrating white South African family that I worked for.

In the United States I visited New York City, Atlanta and Washington, D C. In Tulsa, Oklahoma, I met Native Americans and learnt of the parallels between their history and ours. In Los Angeles I visited Hollywood and Disneyland. I went to San Francisco, where I was struck by physical similarities with Cape Town: vegetation, weather, even the buildings. I went to see the awesome Grand Canyon and made an overnight stop in Las Vegas. That cured me of whatever gambling tendencies might have lurked in my system.

During the trip, I met and talked with people in government, in women's groups, in education, and in the Civil Rights field. I looked at South Africa from a distance, perhaps for the first time dispassionately. I felt such a relief that would be hard to describe.

Dear God! It was not up to me. History would unfold itself in South Africa. The country had already reached a point of no return in the history it would write for itself. It was not up to me.

I had done all I could do, I felt. And I had come to a comforting knowledge: change would come to South Africa.

After my return, all bridge-building stopped for me. I refused speaking engagements. I was not less concerned than I had been before about the fate of the country. In fact, it could be I was more concerned now. But I was tired. Tired of talking to the converted. Tired of talking to stones no amount of talking would ever change. Tired of convincing others I was a human being. If they wanted to know, nothing was stopping them, nothing but themselves.

Social contact of a political kind stopped. I did not even attend the tempting ambassadorial dinners. Not for me the ready excuses of yesterday. I chose to make no exception of their being 'not South African'. I had long known the reason behind my invitation. And it was not my scintillating company or my arresting, irresistible, fascinating wit.

By the end of the year, four short months later, no longer giving speeches had almost killed me. I had become addicted to sharing my views and my reactions to events in the country with others. My splendid isolation felt like a tomb. I desperately needed an outlet for my ideas.

As I listened to or read of events around the country and what was being said about these, I felt I had to respond. Since I had stopped giving talks, I began to write my reactions. Teaching at Herschel also made me realise that I owed this much to myself if no-one else.

If I hadn't known it before, at this school I learned how differently we view certain events, crucial events in our country. For example, on 6 April 1979 – the day the guerrilla fighter Solomon Mahlangu was hanged – a pall of sadness and palpable gloom enveloped the African townships. It was a weekday, a school day. If anyone knew the import of that day where I worked, they certainly kept it to themselves.

Newspaper reports triggered furious responses that I poured onto paper. No inhibitions existed in my new-found place. I didn't have to ask myself, Would such-and-such hurt my friends or my colleagues? The only feelings I took into consideration, the only feelings that mattered, were mine. My feelings, my truth, that was all that concerned me. What a relief!

Once I began writing, I was amazed at how fulfilling an undertaking I found it. Where it lacked the exciting, prickly presence of an audience, it more than compensated with its convenience. I could do it when I had the time. I needed no car, bus or train to get to it. It could be done without interruptions from others. No newspapers could report what I wrote. It was mine. Mine to feel and write what I felt. And to read it again whenever I felt like revisiting those feelings. Newspapers had scared me since the day I gave a speech in Sea Point, saying that it was imperative that black and white find each other for we would have to live in our country together; that no amount of wishing would ever drive the whites into the sea where they would all perish. Well, the next day a newspaper reported this as my wish: that all whites go and drown in the sea.

I was a prolific writer: pages and pages, all in long hand. I couldn't type and had no typewriter. The likelihood of acquiring one was slim.

Sr Aine read some of my musings. She took them with her and typed them. 'You must have these published!' she urged.

Lindy Wilson showed a piece I had written to someone at Ravan Press. She later told me that Ravan Press had expressed interest in a collection of similar work. A person working for a women's magazine in Cape Town saw a pen sketch I had done for a London-based feminist magazine, *Spare Rib*. She actually gave me fifty rand to do more 'township pen sketches'.

Despite such encouragement, I did not embark on a writing career. I did not know I could write. I did not know anyone like me who did. Even the Xhosa writers I knew of were much older, all men, none of whom lived in or near Cape Town. Writing was no less of a myth to me than Icarus and his attempt to reach the sun. Lacking confidence, my writing did not amount to much.

I am convinced my case is not peculiar. What wealth lies buried in our hovels, to be dug up one day? Daily battles just to exist sap energies to an extent hard to imagine. Goals remain goals far too long, perhaps long enough to disappear into vague regrets, frustration and hazy sources of malaise.

As 1979 drew to a lethargic close, despite my misgivings

and yearning, I stuck to my withdrawal from public involvement in Social Responsibility of a political nature. Charity begins at home, I told myself, stifling any regrets. More and more, I directed my energies to coaching UNISA students in Xhosa literature. I had not forgotten how others had helped me to achieve my dream. Moreover, I enjoyed the work and my students were very appreciative.

As was becoming customary in those days, Christmas was half-hearted and fearful. High-school students were still boycotting classes. And as a sign of support, the black people were asked not to take part in the festivities of the season.

Yes, I had disengaged from organisations working for peaceful change or any kind of change. I was tired. I was angry. And I was overwhelmed by the turn of events. I drew little consolation from being proven right. The violence I had predicted had come, all right. What I had not foreseen was its blindness, its lack of discrimination and its openness to exploitation.

'If people are mad enough to want to destroy themselves, fine with me!' I retorted to those who tried to lure me back. I was determined to let things take care of themselves. And they did, in a way that petrified me.

But I couldn't quite stop my silly old heart from caring, from squeezing itself in a teardrop-like spasm each time something awful happened. And awful things were happening with sickening frequency. I had stopped going to meetings. I started holding meetings: my own. Just me and my bleeding heart. Life had gone awry. The country was tearing itself into shreds. The meaning of time had changed. The ordinary year-markers had gone drunk. We no longer observed New Year or Christmas. African school buildings remained empty. School vacations became segregated: holidays were observed at different times for different race groups to accommodate the collapse in black education. Terms were extended or curtailed as a response to students' attendance or absence. White schools remained immune and unaffected.

The schizophrenic split was complete – as if it were not strain enough to move uneasily between the two worlds, black and white. Wake up in Guguletu, fill the eye with rows and rows of same-looking houses. Tread refuse-filled streets on the way to the bus stop. Along the way, dodge storm drains clogged with debris. Arrive at the bus stop and stand in long, listless, lumpish queues. Eventually, the unpredictable and indifferent bus comes. You swarm on. Like a slow take in a movie, the bus chugs along, picking up and dropping off passengers on the way. Then you reach Claremont, your destination. The bus terminus in a business area of the town. Get off. Walk. How many steps? 1,035? Cross over to the highly individual splendour of the other Claremont – far from the pollution-spewing buses by the railway station and far from the invading hordes of servants.

Not a maid, though of that tribe, I come to the white world bringing enlightenment. I teach in a white school. I'm mother of three children. Black, of course. The pain I carry with me whole day long. At work, particularly at work.

It is 1980. All three children are in their teens. Their schooling has come to a stop.

Each morning, I leave three young and healthy people sleeping. They have nothing to do for the whole long day. Even to me it began to look ridiculous, if not downright cruel, to wake them up at the customary hour when they had the whole blessed day to do whatever chores I might delegate.

I would be busy teaching during the day when the irony would assail me: here I was teaching children who came from the *crème de la crème* of white South Africa, and my own three were languishing at home. The young people at Herschel were focused, aggressive in preparing for their future, eager to learn.

Thembeka was eleven when I first gave thought to the

meaning of black parenthood in South Africa. This was in 1974. Out of the pain that realisation had brought came several poems. No doubt, few would agree with me about their poetic merit, but for me these were not just hot thoughts on paper. They were the outpourings of a soul in hell.

I agonised about her future in an untitled poem which went:

> She is eleven,
> I should be in heaven,

and went on to explain why, instead of that state of bliss, I wished I had not had her. For although she had escaped childhood illnesses and the early grave that is the fate of thousands of African infants each year, what was in store for her? What could she aspire to? What would she be allowed to be? The poem ended with an answer to that question. One day, a white woman would say to an old broken Thembeka, 'Thank you, Jane, you've been a good girl.' Dismissing her from service. Dismissing her because, being too old, she no longer coped as efficiently as before. No pension would be hers.

How could I have brought a child into this world, one who could look forward to no better future than that?

This led to another poem, or was it a prose piece? Anyway, it was about the back-to-front arrangement that life is. We choose careers long before we even know who we are, never mind what we are about. What is the use of the wisdom we accumulate after we have bumbled our way through most of our life? The emphasis of this piece was on the unfairness of our biological ripeness coming so much earlier than our mental or intellectual maturing. I had three children. When I had them, what had I known about what having a child meant?

Now, the nightmare returned to haunt me anew.

Before the schools boycott of 1976 we had been able to live in our fool's paradise: were we to receive a good education, we could be something, or so we believed.

Our children were challenging that premise. What education, never mind a 'good' one, can be had with the ratio 480 : 280 : 28? That was government spending in rands on South African children per annum in the order White, Coloured, African.

'Bantu Education cannot be reformed. It must be abolished!' was one of the slogans of those tortured days. All very true. But I had mortgaged my middle age. I did not have a young adulthood. I did not know what it was to be young and carefree. I was a mother at nineteen, a mother of three by age twenty-three, and a no-longer married.

Saddled with children at that tender age, I'd promised myself a second chance. When I'm forty, Sandile will be seventeen, I'd told myself. At that age, with my guidance, he was to have passed matric and, on full scholarship, gone to university. Naturally. And that was to be the beginning of my carefree life, the early adulthood I never had. I had vowed to give myself a fabulous middle age.

But at the rate African education was going, I would be a hundred, I realised, before Sandile finished high school. If he ever did, that is.

Drastic problems call for drastic responses. I decided to flee. Flee my children. Flee the country. Even if it was for only two years. I was battle-weary. And I wasn't even on the battle-front.

A scholarship was offered me. To Cornell. No, I couldn't take it.

Working full-time and part-time, studying by correspondence, I had failed in two important criteria: I did not have enough money to leave for the children and I had failed one of the six papers I was doing for my Honours in Psychology.

How I wept! I needed desperately to run away from my children. I had to flee from the daily reminder that I was raising three people to be locked up, forever, in a poverty that would exceed anything I had known. My dreams of an accomplished offspring lay at my feet, shattered shards on which I was daily forced to tread. I had to find some other life for me and thus for them. Like a miser gone berserk, I spent the whole of 1980 and most of the next year saving rent money and food money for the children. Incidentals would just have to take care of themselves. I was the incurable optimist to the very end.

With my disengagement had come some reticence on my part to be actively involved with students. My own children, as I've said before, were involved only because they were at school. They were the rank and file. As the schools boycotts continued, I began no longer to see eye to eye with most of what was happening.

Why did the protests last the whole year through?

Why were there no alternative projects in place?

If what our children were doing was so correct, why were we not supporting them by refusing to live in segregated neighbourhoods? Why not camp out in tents, away from the townships set aside for the use of black people? Why were we still using our segregated churches, clinics, train carriages? Why not go the whole way, refuse to use any and all segregated facilities and amenities in the country? That would surely be support for the children. That and ensuring they did not lose whole years of study.

My position was that children up to at least Standard Six ought to be allowed to remain in school full-time. From then on, everyone should go on to take correspondence studies. By that time, they would have learnt reading and writing and could thus understand and handle the course material they would receive. This was the option I posed to Bantu Education schools. However, after high school, all those who wanted to go further would boycott the tribal universities. There was the University of South Africa as an alternative. Studies outside the country was another.

To my way of thinking, it was most important that children learn the rudiments. We who supported the students would donate our time and establish enrichment programmes. Those of us gifted in maths could give maths clinics and help students and pupils with the subject. The same would happen with the other subjects as well.

Mine was a voice in the wilderness. A revolution was on. No one wanted to listen to trashy moderation. No one saw any value in evolution. Radical change was the goal. Immediate, radical change. Not gifted in insight, I failed miserably to see how any education, even BAD education, could be so bad that no education might be better.

I made an analogy. One day, I said, it will not surprise me to discover that the schools boycott was orchestrated by people with not the least interest in our advancement. I saw definite similarities between what was happening to us now and what had happened to us in 1857. Then, the AmaXhosa were strong enough to resist colonial coercion to become labourers. A young person, Nongqawuse, told the nation to kill all the cattle and burn all crops. She had received these instructions from 'ancestors', who said that if they were carried out all the white people would be driven into the sea. Today, without government encouragement, African education actually continued to make headway. By 1976 even adult education had reached quite startling levels. Then came the prophecy. Destroy all this enthusiasm, all this progress, and you will be better off. Your situation will improve. In both episodes, we were told to take a leap backwards and were promised undreamt-of advancement. After what came to be known as 'The Cattle-Killing of the Xhosa', a virtual national suicide, the white man had solved his labour problem. We never heard from the 'ancestors' again.

I shudder to think of the terrible waste of human potential that will surely result from today's sacrifice. It will be far worse than anything Bantu Education ever achieved with its own cruel agenda. When these young people who have mortgaged their futures remain perpetually excluded from the economy of the future they are fighting for, where will today's 'ancestors' be? Tell me, I urged, how will a child, fifteen to eighteen years in 1976, ever recoup a decade lost, a decade of no schooling?

No one wanted to listen to that. None among those in the struggle saw such questions as worthy of serious consideration. Had I detected sincerity among the adult supporters of the students, I might have come to the conclusion that it was my inability to see my own limitations that was blinding me. However, to this day, I am not convinced that all those who urged publicly that students should stay away from school until Bantu Education was abolished meant what they said.

Discussing this with fervent supporters of all-out schools boycotts one day, I was accused of having a vested interest. I could not be objective, and that was because of my own children at high-school level: I was allowing my personal situation to cloud the issue.

Another of these friends came right out and asked me if I were on a suicide mission. Didn't I see these children had stopped being reasonable? Did I want my house burnt down?

I am not saying these were not convincing arguments. A colleague had just had her house set alight by the students, her furniture ruined, her house ransacked. And the entire family had had to watch that happening. And to this day, no one who knew this family is sure of exactly how they stood in the way of our liberation. So these were sound arguments. If they didn't dent my mind or move my position, it is not that they were in any way wanting.

But I could not be convinced. I just failed to see how complete illiteracy could be a means to a nation's liberation. Even the friend who hurled 'vested interest' at me was busy with her UNISA studies. Talks with people I once thought I knew and understood plunged me further and further into the dense fog of my bewilderment. Not only was I carrying the burden of knowing others suspected me of alliance with the common enemy, but I did not even have enough survival urge, if not common sense, to go along with the crowd.

Sometimes I actually kid myself that I plan my life. But during those revealing moments when the nakedness of one's existence is laid bare, I know that nothing is further from the truth.

My life, if truth be known, is the result of errors, horrors and coincidence. It is as if to grow, something in my life has to die, to decay, to disintegrate.

I look back on many a tear I have shed. Instead of the sorrow remembered only too well years later, I see in that exact same spot the seed of a flower that later bloomed.

Thus it is that today I am grateful I did not go to Cornell University in Ithaca, New York, though I'd like to visit Cornell one day. After all, it was the first to give me reason to hope, hope that I would make it to an overseas university.

Because I did not go to Cornell in 1980, I went to Columbia University in 1981.

Fifteen

The International Institute of Education or IIE, the organisation in charge of the scholarship programme, was planning for my leaving South Africa in the third week of August. The American school year begins in September. Fine. Except my school year would have reached a crucial point at that time: the matric students would be about to write their last internal examinations, a dress rehearsal for the final in November–December. This put such a strain on me as would be hard to imagine.

There was no doubt in my mind I would leave and do so on schedule. I was equally convinced that this was a dislocation that would be stressful to my students, particularly the matric candidates. Moreover, I was in real fear of notifying the principal, Miss Geldard, of my intention to leave the school. I agonised over the matter, blew it out of all proportion, and nearly drove myself crazy with fear, remorse and doubt.

In the end, sense prevailed. I turned round and told myself the Herschel heavens would not even shake at the departure of an insignificant person like me. If I didn't seize this opportunity, even Miss Geldard would know she had a noodle working for her. Moreover, my students were bright, enthusiastic about Xhosa, had progressed well, and would have little difficulty in the final exams. No, I told myself, I was not crucial to their success at the end of the year, neither was I indispensable.

When the cyclone I'd created in my own mind subsided, I turned to the arrangements I needed to make. Although the children were all in their teens and could look after themselves physically, I still needed the presence of an adult in the house. Of my three sisters, Nomalanga appeared the more suitable: she could be stern when necessary. So I talked to Mother as well as to Nomalanga about her coming to stay at No. 20 during my absence.

To assuage my guilt at leaving the children, I installed electricity in the house, telling myself I was doing so to compensate them for my absence. That cost me about six hundred rand. I bought a fridge. I already had a gas stove: we kept that.

When I told Miss Geldard I was leaving and gave her my reason, she was gracious and practical. She needed a replacement; could I help her find one in the township? All my fears had been for naught. I should have known better. But all my life I have never had the sense of entitlement from which confidence must spring. Whether I acknowledged it openly to myself or not, fact is that for me and many other African women, to be in a job, a good job at that, is more an exception than the rule. Glamorous though this may appear, it is stressful. The incumbent is forever weighed down by the enormous responsibility of being a prototype and role model.

Miss Geldard wanted me to find a replacement. Several women sprang to my mind, foremost Nozipho Ngele (née Sono) and Kuku January, both excellent teachers and well grounded in Xhosa. When they both declined with convincing reasons, I went to another teacher, Lindiwe Duda (now Mrs Siyengo). I had to work hard to convince her it would be to her benefit to leave a secure post in the African schools where her reputation was made and where she was not only accepted but appreciated, and go and teach at a white school in a white suburb. This involves travelling; it involves learning new ways of doing things. But, above all, it entails being the odd one out, the outsider, the foreigner amongst people with a history, a culture and a language dif-

ferent from your own. My desperation giving me uncharacteristic wit and the persuasive skills of a seasoned negotia-
tor, I talked Lindiwe into accepting my proposition. I then
prayed that when she went for the interview, nothing in
what she said or did would upset Miss Geldard. I prayed
even harder that she would not be overwhelmed by the
school until after she had signed the contract. I knew once
that was done, she would do just fine.

Then there were my students to prepare – those who
faced matric exams being foremost in my mind. However, I
was not unconcerned about the others. And once they knew
I was leaving, knew what we had to get done before I left
and why it had to be so, I had their cooperation.

There were also examinations for me to write in preparation for my studies at Columbia: the TOEFL (Test of English
as a Foreign Language) and the GRE (the Graduate Record
Examination).

Finally, there were the children themselves. The decision
to leave them when I did was mine. But I had been pushed
to it. Long ago, when I had thought of studying abroad, it
had always been something I would do after they had left
home and were either at university or working.

Abroad has always meant England for me. I didn't know
of anyone who had gone to the USA to study. However,
when it began to look as if I'd be a hundred before the
eldest passed matric – what with the schools boycotts and
the crisis that plagued Bantu Education – I decided to
change the plan to meet the exigencies of the day.

'Since you have stopped your schooling,' I said to them
one day, 'I am going to continue with mine.' That was when
I'd energetically activated my long-deferred dream and
sought funding to study abroad.

The children and I had discussed my plans, and they did
not voice any misgivings once I let them know there would
be rent money, food money and a little to replace worn
clothing when necessary. About this time, benevolence

smiled and we were favoured with a phone. A phone at N.Y. 74 No. 20 would facilitate communication with the children during my stay in the United States – it was a boon to my plans.

Plans? I suppose the alternate stretches and shrinkings of the earthworm can be called that. I suppose it knows where it is headed, although to me, watching, it looks blind and clumsy, trailing along – painfully slow and uncertain of goal. Let me elevate my own bumblings to the status of plans.

Such were my plans, then, for the children, the house, and outstanding business I was leaving behind as I stepped high, off to New York, in the US of A.

Amidst all this there was Mother. Since Father's death I had been her main source of financial support. Not that she was idle. That word doesn't exist in Mother's vocabulary. But of course, my contribution, unlike her business earnings, was something she could count on at the end of each month.

If Mother was the least bit apprehensive, she kept that well hidden. Mother's enthusiasm for progress, education foremost, is a never-ending source of encouragement to all her children; indeed, to all young people. Her lament – *'Ukuba bendisemtsha! Ngeli lenu ixesha!* – Were I still young. In these times of yours' – speaks volumes. I have heard of parents that are stumbling blocks in the paths of their children. Mother is no such parent. Neither was Father.

Mother's excitement at my pending great adventure knew no bounds. Frequently did she open her mouth on the subject – 'Sindiwe is going to America. Young people! *Yhuu! Abaziyekeli.* They don't sit back.' And if such good fortune could come her daughter's way, why not in the way of others? 'You too should study. See? You could also go to America.' She encouraged those she felt were not using themselves wisely, whether they sought her advice or not.

The mothers of N.Y. 74 came up with a proposal. Wasn't I one of their own children going away? Going to that faraway America they themselves would never see? Well, then, how could they be mothers if they could send their infant away unsuckled *(lungancanciswanga)?* A send-off party was called for. And the mothers of N.Y. 74 donated their baking, cooking and catering skills, and came to be with my family in saying, *'Ndlela-ntle!* Farewell!'

'How can you leave the children?' asked a friend, forcing me to confront a question I had been dodging for a long time. How could I leave the children? I know women who have forgone opportunities to go abroad because they 'couldn't leave their children alone'.

Call it selfishness. Call it dumb. Call it whatever. I just do not see that that is what I did. My children were not being left alone. Mother was a stone's throw away from No. 20, at No. 33. From her gate she can call out and we at No. 20 will hear her call. Nomalanga would move in with my children. There were the neighbours on both sides of me – Mr and Mrs Handula at No. 19 and Mr and Mrs Peters at No. 21 and the Sogiba family at No. 22 – all good people who would not hesitate to step in and help should that become necessary. They had done so since the children were toddlers. Hadn't I been working day in, day out? Never have I had the problem of guilt at being a working mother. What I do will benefit all of us eventually: that has been my guiding principle. I was not leaving them for purely selfish reasons. I had never done that. Always, at the root of most of what I have done were the children. If I became a better anything, wouldn't that make me a better mother? Better able to provide for them? Give them the things they need? And when any rewards have come my way, we have all rejoiced at their coming, certain in the knowledge they were for all of us, the children and me.

What is more, I had no problems about the children's behaviour while I was gone. By this time, it had become quite clear to me that children grow up and become independent of parents. They do as they please. And lucky is the parent whose children's doings coincide with his or her wishes. On the whole, I was lucky, very lucky as a parent.

Of course I helped too. I kept lowering the expectations. The older the children became the less I began expecting of them, in some ways. What I saw children out there do convinced me more and more that I had raised saints. Boys who were holding knives to their parents! Girls who swore at their mothers! With my own eyes, I witnessed young people cause their parents grief, embarrassment and financial hardship – lawyers' fees when a child got himself into trouble with the law, doctor's fees when he got himself knifed in a brawl, compensation to neighbours when he destroyed or stole property belonging to them.

'Not only won't I give a cent of mine to a lawyer, you won't even see me at that trial. Me? I have to go to work to pay the rent and feed you.' I hurled threats at my children, attempting to scare them into lawfulness in case decency had failed to take root.

I held onto the firm belief that I had done what I knew, how I knew it, and to the best of my ability. Now it was up to them. To practise living decently. Without harming themselves.

My powerlessness to give direction to my children had become obvious to me with the growing lack of control we, as parents, exhibited in the townships. Our children had quit school, without so much as 'by your leave'.

I had raised my children alone. Yes, others helped, here and there, but it was understood the children were my responsibility. They knew that. Mother knew that. I knew that. They'd been raised with discipline and love. Now, I told myself, they were old enough to know good from bad. If my training had any effect, they should be able to conduct themselves well in my absence.

'You know what I expect of you,' I said to them. 'You know what is right and you know what is not right.' Children were busy ruining their lives, with their parents watching, too powerless to stop the train to hell.

'If you choose to do things you know I wouldn't have approved of, that is up to you. But remember this: you, each one of you, can hurt me by what you do. But my hurt is for you. It is the hurt of a parent for the loved child. There is one thing you must remember though; nothing you do can hurt me more than it will hurt you.'

What more could I say? That I was bewildered? Afraid? Floundering in this reversal of roles, experiencing loss of control? How could I saddle my poor children with all the fear shredding my guts?

'People say I'm an informer and I don't know how to make them believe I'm not'? Atrocious. What could they say in return?

'I'm tired. I've been working for almost twenty years and have nothing to show for it. And I fear if I work for twenty more years there will still be nothing to show for it'? What was I sowing: aimless living? Why should they ever stir themselves if I told them there was no reward? Or, 'I'm tired of being responsible for so many people in so many ways'? Where would I be, saying that these people should go? Who should they depend on? Welfare? Or, 'I am too weak to wean myself from a relationship both ruinous and addictive'?

I said none of these things. My children, I believed, thought of me as strong, self-sufficient, focused. I couldn't find it in my heart to disillusion them at that point. They were still young. Later, soon enough, they would get to know what a scared rabbit I am.

Farewell parties and speeches done, I busied myself with the painful but inevitable last-minute shopping and tying of loose ends. At last, the day had come.

I left South Africa on a Sunday, 23 August. The year was 1981. After a long but uneventful flight, we landed at J F Kennedy Airport at seven o'clock in the morning. A Monday.

This was my second visit to the United States. On my

first, I had been met at the airport and, until I left the country, provided with an escort. Now I was very much on my own. From the airport, I took a taxi straight to Columbia University's School of Social Work.

Yes, I was going to do a Master's degree in Social Work. After a careful weighing up of my options, I had decided I would not want to go back to teaching, particularly in African schools. What was happening in those schools was just too heart-rending for me to want to be part of it. And I was pessimistic then about any chance for change there. There were not many white schools that employed Xhosa teachers. I had been exceedingly lucky to get the position at Herschel. Realistically, I could not expect such a fluke to repeat itself. In one life?

Finally, I settled on Social Work. Not because I had forgotten my earlier reservations or revised my opinion of social work and its import for black lives. No. But I had a plan.

I would do a combined degree at the School of Social Work with a minor in Business from the Columbia Graduate School of Business. The latter qualification I would use to get a job in industry. A well-paying job. I would make good money upon my return. I saw myself in some personnel function of a large company. And the social work? Well, that was to be for my Social Responsibility.

At the School of Social Work I had chosen Organisational Development as my platform or area of specialisation. With the numerous organisations back home, I knew I would find a way of using the skills, knowledge and training this course offered. I had watched this arrangement in white families. Husband and wife would sometimes decide on this arrangement: one worked and earned the family's livelihood while the other donated his or her services. The obvious advantage in this arrangement is that there is money on which to live – and live well – since whites are generally well qualified in whatever they do. Another advantage, and one I'd totally missed until a spouse in such an arrangement pointed it out to me, is that one parent was left 'untainted' as far as the police were concerned. Social Responsibility almost always incurred the wrath of the police. Therefore, should the police want to flex their muscles, knock down or arrest some 'do-gooders', the working spouse was safe. One of the parents was there for the children.

For me, being alone, the situation wasn't quite that free of complications. However, the idea of separating my social responsibility from my earning capability appealed enormously to me. All the jobs I had done – those with even a hint of being 'humanitarian' – tended to pay peanuts. I wasn't getting any younger, I told myself; it was time I started making real money.

To those who tried to con me into guilt about deserting the sinking ship of Bantu Education, I haughtily retorted, 'I have taught African children for more than five years. If I've been any good, good should come of it. If, on the other hand, I have been a bad teacher, then I've caused enough harm already. Let those I've taught take on from here. Who said teaching had to be a life-time sentence?'

The taxi deposited me in front of the School of Social Work a little before 8.30 a.m. – too early for the faculty to have come. The grey building seemed stony and forbidding, a thing apart from the warm and encouraging letters I had received. It was difficult to associate those letters with the cold grey staring unsmilingly at me.

I looked up the street and found myself dwarfed by the buildings on both sides. Like a midget in a tunnel, I felt myself pressed in and reduced to insignificance. The suitcases at my feet were suddenly too large for me to drag.

The door was locked and didn't yield to my fumblings. And then I saw a stirring inside: through the glass doors, a woman waved enquiringly. I pointed to my suitcases thinking, Aha! Someone is here to meet me. It had seemed strange to me that the school would have neglected me in that way.

When the woman I had seen opened the door and found out I was a foreign student, she helped me drag my suitcases inside and told me, 'You'll have to wait for Dean Reed. She should be here in a few minutes.'

We shook hands as I gave her my name: Sindiwe Magona. I had made yet another decision. I would give myself a fresh start here where nobody knew my name.

At home, most people called me Sindi which, in Xhosa, sounds quite different from Cindy. Truly speaking, however, neither is my name. Here, I would insist that my full name be used. 'Sindiwe as in *Cindy we[nt]* to town' – I'd explain to anyone who looked perplexed at hearing the name for the first time. But I wouldn't tell anyone not to take the trouble to say my name, to use an abbreviation instead. Oh no. I'd done that long enough.

Dean Reed duly arrived and we went to her office. There she explained to me that most of the students and faculty were away. This was summer vacation, just before the Fall Semester began.

I had no address, nowhere to stay. I had gaily assumed the school would house me. Things were a little more complicated than that, I learned. The school and the Housing Section have very little to do with each other.

That first morning, Dean Reed helped me to get settled. Without batting an eyelid, as if students arrived in taxifuls at the school, suitcases in tow, every other day of the week, she made my action look so commonplace that it wasn't until much later that I realised how far from usual it was.

'Let me see if Erlin, a student from Uganda, is in. She is the president of the Foreign Students' Caucus.' Dean Reed dialled, spoke to someone on the phone and replaced the receiver. 'She'll be here in ten minutes. Her name is Erlin Ibreck,' she said, writing the name down for me.

We had not finished our cups of coffee when Erlin arrived. In what I would later learn was atypical of New

York City, Erlin literally took me by the hand and helped me get organised.

First, we went to the bank as I had very little American currency. From the bank we went house-hunting. Erlin used the phone and, after several tries, told me there was room at International House. The name sounded exciting, dynamic and pregnant with possibility.

By the time Erlin and I parted, we had had a meal at a diner, she had helped me open a bank account, find accommodation, unpack some of the things I would need during the day, shown me round International House, and helped me in a host of other ways that now escape my memory. Along Broadway, we had met the occasional student and I had been introduced.

After making sure I would be okay, Erlin finally left me to myself. We had been together for more than six hours, I think. That was the beginning of a friendship that has lasted to this day.

I had left South Africa thoroughly fed up with the state that the country was in, disillusioned with its humanity so lacking in humaneness, chagrined at some of my white friends and acquaintances. In America, I told myself, I will steer clear of South African whites. The ones I already know at home are enough. I am not going to the United States to find South African friends, especially whites.

Imagine my disquiet when I discover in my class another South African. White, naturally, and all of twenty-five years of age. Fuming, I asked myself, 'Is there no escape, no relief from this nuisance? Is no place far enough for me to hide?' Added to this young woman's presence, a fact irritating enough to me, was her age, a perpetual reminder of my being bonzai'd. Yes, we were in the same programme, both of us doing a Master's degree in Social Work. She was more than ten years younger than I was. How come it had taken me so much longer to arrive at the same point? It helped little that Moira (as we shall call her) was eager to befriend her compatriot. 'Aha!' the cynic told herself, '*Now*, she wants to know you. But what happens when you get back? Can you see her inviting you to her posh home?' No, I vowed, I would have as little to do with Moira as possible.

In the same way, International House turned out to be an unfortunate choice. I had fled South Africa truly done with building bridges. I didn't care if the whole nation drowned in what I saw as its self-made sea of bigotry. 'If they are mad enough to want to destroy everything, themselves included … well, far be it from me to stop them.' I can't recall now when I had come to the conclusion that the fate of the entire country rested on my shoulders. But putting that burden down was a relief. And I did not do that any too soon.

At International House, the philosophy of the brotherhood of man was espoused. Smiles, handshakes and introductions were expected as a matter of course. But my cheeks were still sore and my lips cracked from all the smiling I had done back home while building bridges. And so, in the midst of this spirit of oneness, I stood apart, disgruntled, unhappy and sour.

The beginning of classes brought with it a whole bag of problems. Part of the Master's programme involves serving an internship, or field work as it is called. Three days a week in my first year of study, I went to the South Bronx. This meant taking the subway there and back.

The subway is for the most part an underground train. Fast, noisy, graffiti-decorated. My greatest fear in using it was losing my way underground. I am a land animal. The mole mode of living is definitely not for me.

Helpful New Yorkers just confused me even more than the subway. When eventually I found myself up on sun-lit land, firm cement with white markings telling me where the middle of the road was, corners clearly demarcated, I'd ask someone, 'Which way is —?', and get the nonchalant answer, 'Uptown, two blocks.'

Blocks, to me, meant buildings. It took months before I

read the new meaning here: corner to corner. But the more confounding piece of information to unscramble was 'up-town' and 'downtown'.

'Up' to me indicated an incline. If you are village-born, when someone gives you directions and says 'up' or 'down', that is exactly what they mean. Up. Down. That is the lie of the land.

Well, not eager to exhibit my being a Johnny-come-lately, and a dimwitted one at that, I wouldn't ask, 'How now, since as far as the eye can see the ground is flat, level?' But I did use my own two eyes to try to discern even the slightest rise or dip. No. The streets round the campus remained stubbornly flat despite my exaggerated detection skills.

When in exasperation I asked Erlin about the mystery, the answer was so simple, so easy, even I could have come up with it unaided. Of course! Why hadn't I guessed it? Up-town, as the street numbers rose. Downtown, as they decreased. How marvellously convenient.

I had not been in New York a month when the different cultural mores hit me. 'No, Sindiwe, here women don't hold hands.' I had pushed Erlin to verbal explanation. She had been telling me in so many subtle ways not to hold hands with her or, worse, put my arm around her waist as we walked up and down Broadway.

I'd put down her reticence to her English upbringing, for although she is Ugandan, Erlin grew up in England. I, wholly African, was going to teach her the unbridled warmth of friendship – woman to woman.

At home, there was absolutely nothing sexual about women holding hands. I grew up doing that. And even now, when I am home, in the city or away in the village, I do it and feel no awkwardness whatsoever. Erlin's enlighten-ment threw me to the ground: 'People will think we are lesbians.'

Well, well, well! We certainly didn't want that, did we? From then on, each time I touched Erlin or, as I met and got to know more people, another woman, my hand would re-coil as if it had found itself clasping a live cobra. However, until I left Columbia University and the City of New York, I still found that on occasion I'd forget myself and take an-other woman's hand in mine. Old habits die hard.

I was certainly in a different world; 'Miss! Miss! Excuse me, Miss, you dropped your scarf!' That person would pay dearly for his or her pains in trying to help me. Miss? Not in the habit of being addressed with common civility, I found it took a long time before it dawned on me that I might be the person thus addressed. 'Hey! What do *you* want? *Wat soek hierdie ding hier? Ja! Vroumens! Mama. Kaffir.*' Those and other epithets were my name where I came from. 'Madam, Miss, Lady' – those turned my head round only so that I could see who was thus addressed. But I got used to them as if, all my life, I'd just been waiting for the world to right itself, and finally it had.

I stayed in International House one month only. The room was small and overpriced. I hated the ambience of over-friendliness and 'let's get to know each other', finding it artificial and contrived.

Johnson Hall, a Columbia University dormitory, was, like International House, full of young people. Some were barely out of their teens. For the first time, it occurred to me that I was no longer young. These young people annoyed me, fre-quently and unerringly. They were loud. Their dress too flip-pant. In the dormitories, they played their stereos incessantly and at eardrum-splitting decibels. In short, everything about them irritated me. I was of a different season, a different harvest. They were young. I was not.

I began to miss the children I had left with such light-heartedness. A little. I had told myself I wouldn't see them for almost two years, told myself I wouldn't pine for them. They would be fine. And two years would pass by swiftly and before they really missed me. And I actually believed what I had told myself.

Perhaps I didn't. I don't know. But when, after a month, I left Johnson Hall having secured a studio apartment (likewise Columbia University housing), I had cause to think of my children fondly. And yes, with some misgivings that we were not together. But perhaps this does not count as missing them, perhaps it is just one more indication of my selfishness.

Now that I had what I'd wanted, living by myself, another problem arose. Until I lived in this studio, I had never ever had a room which I would be the only one to sleep in, to wake up there in the morning, alone – always alone; to cook, eat, wash up dishes and put them away – alone. Iron clothes, hang them up or put them into drawers – alone. Read, study, listen to the radio or watch television – alone. Always I'd had someone with me – child or children, younger siblings, lover, friend.... Even at Fezeka, in the room I'd been given, there were people ... in and out, night and day. But now I was all alone.

Absolutely petrified, I saw how insignificant my newfound independent living made me. I was nobody. I counted for nothing. No one knew when I was having a bad night. And no one cared.

I had not realised that part of my identity was those others, significant in my life. In the townships I am known as Thembeka's mother, Thoko's mother, Sandile's mother or *Sisi* of any of my five younger siblings: Mawethu, Sizeka, Nomalanga, Nomduzana, and Thembani. I am also known as MaNtumbeza's daughter. Here people only knew me as Sindiwe.

This sense of dislocation hit me hard. It was as if someone had just come and taken away my face, and left my head in its place fronted by some featureless blob. That could hardly be said to be me.

At home, when I had a slight headache, my mother cackled around me like an anxious mother-hen: 'If you plonk your behinds down instead of running to the shops to get her pain tablets, what do you all think you'll eat if she dies?' – goading any of my sisters and brothers to action. But here no one would know if I were dying from severe stroke or haemorrhage. I'm not saying that my family's consideration sounded like evidence of great love. But, hey, it said I was needed, perhaps even appreciated. That is more than could be said of my situation in New York City. Here no one would miss me the next morning if I died during the night. Stench from my decomposed body would alert neighbours, days later, that something was wrong. This realisation put such a fear in my heart that I dragged poor Erlin into an arrangement.

At least once a day we called each other. Even a Scotch ring was reassuring. She'd let the phone ring twice and replace the receiver. And I'd do the same. That said we were okay and goodnight. It not only kept me sane but increased my appreciation of my children and my family. These were the people with whom I identified myself. They gave meaning to the life I lived, the me I knew, and whatever tranquillity I enjoyed. My gratitude to my family threatened to choke me. They had given me so much, loved me so much, asked for so little in return. And I had not appreciated their contribution to my general well-being.

The bliss of having real teachers was not all I had anticipated. UNISA lecturers visited major centres in South Africa once or twice a year. And I know that students looked forward to the visits. The Columbia experience, I had imagined, would be a feast, like these UNISA visits, only almost daily. Luxury!

Well, interpersonal interaction between students and teacher, between students and between members of a caucus were not always friendly, pleasant or constructive. As with all human interaction, friction, misunderstandings and antipathy arose, dampening my much-looked-forward-to 'real student' experience. I had not bargained on dealing with pettiness, laziness, intellectual jealousies, competition and all these rather untidy human feelings. I had come looking for a clean, comfortable, learning environment, forgetting the other aspects of being human.

However, there was a funny side to being part of a student body on campus. By the middle of the first year I no longer went to my closet frantic with worry about what I would wear. I knew by then that 'See you later' didn't mean I had a date, just as 'Let's have lunch' or 'Let's have dinner' was not an invitation to someone's house for a meal. It could lead to one of the cafeterias on and around campus, an eatery or a restaurant, where each person paid for herself. But, then again, it could lead to absolutely nothing at all.

When people heard my field work was in the Bronx, the South Bronx, most were appalled. The South Bronx is where the movie *Fort Apache* was filmed. It has a reputation of being extremely dangerous. It looks it. Walking down some of the streets, one can easily imagine oneself in some war-devastated zone. The South Bronx has not healed from the riots of thirty years ago. Buildings stand staring out blindly, windows gouged out, without soul or substance. Some have been taken over by drug pedlars and converted into drug dens where people congregate to get a quick fix.

But I had no sense that I was at greater risk in the South Bronx than I was anywhere else in New York. Perhaps this has something to do with the report I happened to hear in my first week in New York.

I was listening to the news, something I know better than to do first thing in the morning now, for it can colour one's day a dark, sinister, grey-black all day long. This day, new in the city, I thought I'd heard wrong. The announcer, fortunately, repeated the news item: a woman sitting on a bench in Central Park had been shot dead. Not without the perpetrator of the crime giving a reason: 'I don't like your face.'

That is all the man said before pulling out a gun and blowing half the woman's face away. Central Park is far from the South Bronx. From that day, lacking a face that would launch even one ship, I fixed it in my mind that New York was a very, very dangerous place. That I should learn to make my face appear as insignificant, blank and devoid of expression as if it *were* already dead. Perhaps, then, no one would want to speed it on its way to the next world.

News from home was not encouraging. I had been in the United States less than three months when problems began. Calling home one evening, the phone rang and rang and rang, to my growing alarm. Only death could empty the house in Guguletu of everyone living there. All through the night, I called my telephone number. No one picked up.

The next evening, confronted with the same results, I called a nearby friend in Cape Town and was told my phone had been disconnected. So soon had my plans already gone awry. Even as I frantically tried to understand reason, my house of cards was falling apart.

Moira did not endear herself to me by being able to go home for Christmas. Envy sat at the back of my throat like a sharp-clawed crab, slowly nibbling away at what little remained of my common sense and sense of fair play. Why? It was as if the poor child had stolen money from my purse. That is how I resented her – showing me so vividly what I could never be, what I could never have.

And I wasn't doing that badly myself. Indeed, I had never had it so good in my entire life, as far as money was concerned.

While other students complained, irked by the straits of the life of a student, I beamed from ear to ear. My stipend of a little over five hundred dollars a month left me with a little under two hundred dollars after I'd paid my rent. Never had I had so much money at my disposal.

Once I'd overcome the fear of living alone, my accommodation was sheer luxury. A shower with hot and cold water. A kitchenette, complete with stove and fridge. What more could I ask for? The studio had electricity. Making a cup of tea or coffee was no longer a test of endurance: unruly flame threatening to hit the ceiling and set the house on fire. No more primus stove. No more paraffin with its nostril-plugging fumes. Clean gas. I had no reason to complain. My only regret? That I had not stumbled on this way of life earlier in my existence. Had I known, I'd have been a student, abroad on a scholarship, from age twenty to forty. I can think of no more pleasant, stress-free way of spending one's early and middle years.

And then the school year was over. Erlin graduated and, of course, I went to her graduation. I would be a second-year and final-year student, come September. Meanwhile, there was the summer to enjoy. Hot. Sticky. Humid. But miles and miles of time. And loads of things to do, some even free.

Before the year's end IIE invited all the students that had come aboard its programme in 1981 to a reunion that was held at one of Manhattan's posh hotels. Students came from all over the United States. We had been notified that government representatives from our countries would attend, and seating would be arranged by country. But I – disclaimed by South Africa and not exactly honoured by the Transkeian citizenship that had been thrust into my hands – assumed that IIE was aware of all this and would invite neither party. Imagine my surprise, therefore, when I found not one but two men waiting for me: my representatives!

'Oh, here she is!' I hear one say as I step out of a cab. It was a wet day and I was running late. At the entrance to the hotel, I am met by three men. The gentleman from the sponsor introduces himself and then proceeds to tell me: 'And these two gentlemen are from your country.' Afrikaner, large and clear, is written on each of the two faces looking at me beamingly. And one of these men is Mr Van der Merwe, *nogal* [on top of it]!

Even as we make our way to the table where a little South African flag stands, my mind is working like crazy. How could IIE have done this? And how could the South African Consulate respond to the invitation? After all, they needed just to look at my name to know. Sindiwe Magona can be nothing but African, or 'Bantu' according to their designation; someone they had decided was not South African. In addition, a simple check on whether I carried one of their passports would have told them I was one of their discarded. Surely that was not such a difficult thing to do?

But now we were sitting round a small table. All round the vast room, gay mini-flags gently waved on each table. Students, singly or in twos and threes, sat chatting to officials from their countries.

Maybe I should have flounced out of that hotel – preferably after a heated speech denouncing the two impostors. Or perhaps a more telling act would have been to wait until the main course was on the table and then letting fly. How dared they?

I sat there, too numb to think straight; my addled brain could not tell me what to do. I sat there, a polite smile pasted on my face. I listened to Mr Van der Merwe compliment me on my achievement – being a Master's student, having toiled long and hard, studying by correspondence from matric. 'You see,' he enthused, 'in our country it is still possible to pull yourself up by your bootstraps. Unlike this country, where everything is given to you on a platter!' I did not tell him that I had had no boots, never mind bootstraps.

I began the second year on a high note. I was elected president of the Foreign Students' Caucus. I had met all the requirements of my first year, passed everything with nothing deferred, nothing incomplete.

My anxiety about going back to South Africa without a firm job offer seemed to have paid off. I'd sent off dozens of letters to American companies with subsidiaries in South Africa. Reluctantly, the School of Social Work had agreed to use a pharmaceutical company, RR&K, as my field-work placement. There had been a hitch: I would not be under the direct supervision of a qualified social worker. However, RR&K found someone within the organisation and he agreed to oversee my internship. I was placed in the office of Equal Opportunity.

The understanding was that I was being prepared, groomed if you will, for a position with RR&K (South Africa) in Personnel. However, management at Headquarters made it quite clear that this decision was not up to them. They did not, could not and would not hire for their branches.

Fortunately, two managers from RR&K (South Africa) were scheduled to visit Headquarters at different times in the course of the year, and I was promised interviews with them. Everyone at Headquarters thought I would be suitable for a position with their company. The company prides itself as a leader in the area of equal opportunity, and helping the South African subsidiary uphold this image was not un-important to Headquarters.

I had started the job hunt a full year before time because of one reason: fear. Since I hoped to work in industry, rather than return to South Africa and begin job-hunting there, I felt more confident of getting decent treatment in the United States. The parent companies were having a hard time justifying their presence in South Africa. In the United States these companies faced growing demands that they quit that country. Part of their defence was that their pres-ence in South Africa gave blacks job opportunities they would not otherwise get. They were anxious to prove this by employing educated black South Africans or, at least, dis-covering these for their South African subsidiaries.

Well, a good number of them forgot my address. Not all

the companies I'd written to even bothered to reply to my letters. Of the four who did, only RR&K offered a slim chance – an interview to see whether something could be arranged. They were not promising me anything either.

However, after the interview things began to look promising. And when eventually the Columbia School of Social Work felt its requirements were met, I was all set up. And then, surprise! I would be paid a full professional's salary for the hours I worked at RR&K as an intern.

I had not banked on a paid internship. A few of the students at school had field-work placements that paid them something – not much, from what I gathered. But to most students, even a little is much appreciated.

Here I'd been thinking I had a pretty good arrangement with just my stipend. Now, with the RR&K 'salary', I was loaded. I had come to the United States leaving barely enough to cover the most basic needs of my children. Now, suddenly, I was in a much better position than I had anticipated. Could it get any better?

It never rains but pours: and we all see disaster. Well, rain can be a blessing, as we all know. And at the beginning of 1982, it looked as if it would never stop. My sky had opened up and it looked as if it would always be kind.

I had met Julian de Wet during my 1978 visit to the United States. Upon my return three years later, we had renewed our acquaintance because he did not live far from Columbia University campus. Julian is originally from Wynberg, a suburb of Cape Town, but now works at the United Nations in New York. In February 1982, he called me and we made an appointment to meet.

After the 'hellos and how are you's', he came to the point:

'You know, your English is good....' True to nature, I wouldn't let him go any further. Praise always makes me uncomfortable. No one would ever guess how I thrive on it.

'Oh, no!' I gasped.

'Oh, it's true. Your English is very good.' He was not going to be side-tracked by a silly show of false modesty. 'You must know that,' he added, the slightest hint of a smile around his lips. His eyes, however, were twinkling merrily.

When we were through with the cackle, Julian told me there was a vacancy in his unit. They were looking for a Xhosa-speaker who had a good command of English. It was a part-time position.

Me? Work at the United Nations? This time, no false sense of anything provoked the response: 'I don't think so!' I just couldn't see anything like me crawling into such an august body. That the qualifications the job called for were ones I could in all modesty say I possess and perform very well ... still, that didn't embolden me to link myself with the World Body. No. Not me. Me? At the United Nations?

Thank Almighty God and the ancestors, Julian swept my silly protestations aside and arranged for me to go to the United Nations and meet the relevant official. The happy result? For the last three months of my stay in the United States, I had a part-time job with the United Nations.

Such a windfall was certainly nothing I had banked on. I sent birthday gifts. I sent extra money home. I was even able to save.

Yes, I was doing a lot. But New York City is a very busy place; it fosters a spirit of daring. 'Do,' it says, showing you the rewards of those who have done. 'Dare!' it shouts from the rooftops of its skyscrapers. For more than a decade my life had been busy. And so, what was burdensome about studying full-time, serving an internship three days a week, and going to the United Nations once a week?

And there was a sense of calm that came from the distance I enjoyed away from the burning issues of South Africa. Yes, I saw poverty in New York: homeless people, utterly destitute, sleeping on ice-covered pavements in winter. With their torn clothes and filthy blankets between them and a frozen death. Reports of child-stealing, child molestation and infanticide were disquieting. Black men were said to be an endangered species: 'They're all in jail or they are on drugs or they are homosexuals,' said a young woman lamenting the scarcity of young men, eligible men. And I've heard her cry echoed by others on TV – by mothers who've lost sons to drugs, fathers who no longer recall the faces of their sons, kidnapped by a life of crime and the prison system, by drugs, poverty and shame-tinted illnesses that, instead of evoking family support, all too often arouse anger, accusations and recriminations.

I learnt of the anger of the African American: a deep-seated, smouldering anger born of a sense of betrayal, a promise not fulfilled.

Where I come from, the experience of the African American is glamorised, held up as an ideal, an example of the progress possible under ideal, auspicious circumstances. In the United States, the picture is not quite that clear, not that simple, and far from glamorous. The African American I meet, listen to on TV and read about does not parade about as the subject of a beneficial system of government. Far from it.

Despite the great upheavals of the 1960s in American history, despite the sacrifices of the black people in the quest for real freedom, despite Supreme Court decisions enforcing and entrenching their civil rights, those civil rights continue to be elusive. They are still out of reach for the black man, woman and child in the United States of America. They continue to be not only violated but eroded.

I watched and thought. The realisation of the enormity of what had been done to these people shook me to the core. A great fear takes hold of me. In the sorry plight of Afro-America's today, I see my tomorrow: the plight of the African in South Africa in years to come.

I often pray that my insights and my fears are unfounded, an error of judgement. Never before have I prayed so hard, so sincerely. Please, dear God, as apartheid crumbles, wipe away the scars of the past. Empower those who have suffered. Let them outgrow the hurt done them. Let them flourish from even such a crushed, emaciated past as theirs. Let them grow, despite the fact of their having been deliberately stunted for centuries.

What is good fortune, extreme good fortune, if it touches no-one else but oneself? I brought both Mother and Thembeka to my graduation in May.

Of course, I wished I could bring everybody. But poor Thembeka was the one who had attempted to sit for the matric exams twice without success. I blamed the chaos in black education; with such uncertainty, I felt sorry for her. And Mother? Mother would be able to see the apple of her eye, Jongi, after two years shy of two decades since she would go via London. At my graduation, Mother, the eldest female child in her family, stood tall besides my eldest, Thembeka. I am Mother's eldest daughter too. We are a weepy family, and for some strange reason we weep more copiously when overjoyed. All three of us were red-eyed by the end of the day.

There was talk of a more permanent position at the United Nations. I waited nearly two months. After three applications for visa extensions, granted for a month at a time, I decided it was time to go home. After the intensity of studying, the internship and the part-time job at the United Nations, the waiting jarred. The lack of structure in my day unsettled me, made me yearn for the country I had ached so badly to leave. I began to miss my two other children and the rest of my family.

Besides, I had to hurry home. My youngest brother, Thembani Matolo, was coming out of circumcision. I had to be there for his coming-out ceremony. As it is, he'd done this a year later to accommodate me. I had to be there.

I arrived back in South Africa in the last week of July. So

much had changed. So much remained the same.

It was at the point of entry that I was reminded of where I had returned to: the lies, the myths, the distortion, the humiliation. All these began right there at the Customs Office, Jan Smuts Airport, Johannesburg.

Welkom na Suid-Afrika! Welcome to South Africa! blazed the billboards. We walked, a confused straying huddled bunch, just spewed out by the plane. We walked into the terminal building.

South African Citizens ... *Aliens* ... the signs above the counters shouted. I fell in line behind other foreigners. Verily, I was back home.

Slowly the line snaked forward in involuntary jerks and shuffles, breaks and rearrangements. I inched forward like a segment of a serpent, propelled by those behind me and pulled by those ahead of me. I do not know how the other foreigners felt. I was frozen, quivering jelly inside.

Finally, my turn. The burly Afrikaner extended a fleshy hand. I let go of the passport, the document denouncing me as a citizen of Transkei. This was the second trip I was making using this perverted passport. So I was slightly better prepared than the first time. I was travelling on a passport no other country in the world recognised except, of course, South Africa, the country that had sired these homelands. My visa to any country abroad was on a separate piece of paper, as no country would defile its official stamp by affixing it to the passport of the 'Transkei'. However, I did not put it past the mentality of the Afrikaners at customs to blame me, harass me, for the passport being clean, innocent of any stamps from foreign lands.

'Vertrek / Left 1981-08-23' was the last endorsement in my passport. I was at the border post. The customs official was stamping right under that very endorsement 1983-07-27, the date of my return. He pushed the passport back towards me.

If any incongruity struck him, I failed to detect it in his face.

Sixteen

I returned home triumphant. I was a graduate of an Ivy League College in the United States. I had a Master's degree. I had a job offer. Life looked good.

Thembani's coming-out ceremony was within days of my arrival. Although mishaps are not common, it is still a relief when the initiates return hale, for injuries and even deaths have been known to happen in the 'bush'. The celebrations lasted the whole weekend.

I turned my mind to East London, to RR&K and the job I was about to start.

The arrangement I had made with Mr Trollop, one of the two managers who had come to Headquarters whilst I was serving an internship there, was that upon my return I would phone the company. Mr Trollop had given me his business card saying, 'Call reverse charges. I'll alert my secretary to expect your call.'

Later, he had sent me the RR&K (South Africa) newsletter to 'familiarise' me with some of the goings-on there.

We were no longer on the phone since mine had been disconnected not long after my departure. That didn't bother me much. Had Mr Trollop, who understood how hard life was for a black person in the country, not asked me to reverse charges? All I needed, therefore, was a phone; he would accept the charges. I went to a friend's home nearby. No problem, I could use her phone.

'Could I speak to Mr Trollop?'

'Who shall I say is calling?'

Oh, I thought, this must be his secretary. She is expecting

my call. Confidently, 'Oh, this is Sindiwe Magona. I'm calling from Cape Town.'

'Can you spell that for me? What is it in connection with?'

This doesn't sound like someone who's been alerted to the possibility of my calling. Think. Fast. 'He asked me to call him. We met when he was in the United States.'

'Please hold.' … 'Hello? I'm sorry, but Mr Trollop is in a meeting.'

'May I leave a message? Hearing a *mmh-mmh*, I went on, 'Please give him this number.' I rattled off my friend's number and specified, 'I'll wait for Mr Trollop's call tomorrow morning between nine and half past nine.'

The next morning I was at my friend's house long before nine, in case Mr Trollop had a busy schedule and called the number earlier than requested.

By half past twelve, he still had not called. I left. Sharp at nine the next morning, however, I was back waiting. Just in case. I did this for a week and then risked another call. Mr Trollop had gone to a conference and wouldn't be back for two weeks. I left a message for him please to contact me: same number, same time, exactly two weeks from the day I left the message.

On that day, the call came promptly at the stroke of nine. We exchanged greetings, made small talk, and then Mr Trollop apologised that he'd been so difficult to get hold of. He added, 'We are sending you a ticket to fly up here. How is Friday for you? Plan to spend the whole day.'

Friday was fine with me. And so, three days after talking to Mr Trollop, I was on my way to RR&K in East London.

My pre-paid ticket awaited me at the airport. An hour or so after leaving Cape Town, we were in East London.

There was Mr Trollop's secretary to pick me up and drive me to the offices. A beaming Mr Trollop met me as I walked into the building. In his office there were two people, a man and a woman: Africans.

For the whole day, these two people drove me around

Mdantsane, the township close to East London where I would live. They had been told to show me the township and its facilities. For lunch we went outside Mdantsane to a posh restaurant. Again, this was part of the day's plan. Eventually, we returned to the plant, tired. It was about five o'clock: going home time. I had a plane to catch at seven.

My escorts deposited me at Mr Trollop's office where he was waiting. They said their goodbyes and after expressing the hope they would see me again, they left. I had no doubt they would see me again. We would be working for the same company, soon.

'We-ll?' That was Mr Trollop asking for my verdict, my decision. Was I taking the job? Now that I'd seen what relocation would spell for me and the children, did I still want to go through with it? Leave Cape Town and come to work in East London?

'I'll take it.'

The man burst into tears. 'O my God, Sindiwe. O God!' Something was wrong. Very, very wrong. I stood there waiting, dumb.

Mr Trollop's face was beetroot red. His eyes were glassy and he was busy mopping his crumpled face with a big white handkerchief. 'I don't have a job to offer you, Sindiwe.' Ice replaced all the blood in my veins.

I listened, numbed beyond feeling. I listened to a story gone all wrong. This was not supposed to be happening. There was a mistake. I had a job.

But the man who'd flopped into a chair waving me to another was saying: 'We are facing litigation. So we have no money to pay you. I am sorry, Sindiwe.'

An additional problem, said Mr Trollop, was that the company had employed a lot of reactionary whites who had fled newly independent Zimbabwe. He was not at all sure how they would react to my working there.

Mr Trollop presented such a picture of suffering that I could not but sympathise with him. And he in turn softened the blow by telling me: 'With your qualifications, I'm sure someone will snatch you up pretty soon. Don't hesitate to use my name for reference.'

I couldn't fault him. He was concern itself: 'And I don't know how I'll do this, but I'm going to talk to someone higher up. I'll suggest that we give you a little something. Just to tide you over, nothing much. Until you find yourself a job.'

What was there to say? We shook hands and he showed me to another car in which someone else was waiting to drive me to the airport. It was not until we were descending to land at Cape Town that the full impact of Mr Trollop's words hit me. I was jobless.

The man had flown me all the way from Cape Town to East London. There a company car and two smiling company servants were put at my disposal to 'show me round'. I had spent a whole day going through an exercise he knew was futile. Mr Trollop said that he had hoped I would be so appalled by the conditions I saw in Mdantsane that I would turn the job 'offer' down.

Feeble reasoning on his part, of course. Why would the conditions in Mdantsane disgust me more than those in Guguletu? Or was this gentleman assuming I would compare Mdantsane with New York? Did it not occur to him that South African blacks are king at the art of adjustment? That we learn to live like ordinary human beings when in other countries and know we will live under subhuman conditions when we are back home?

What choice did I have now? I had given up the United Nations job by the time I left New York. RR&K had come to nothing; even the compensation hinted at during my final meeting never materialised. But then I had been told the company was going through a hard time. Tell me about it. Tell me about hard times. And this time, even I was too ashamed to ask anybody for help. People were expecting great things from me, with my Master's degree from

Columbia University.

Panic-stricken, I began job-hunting. Precisely what I had wanted to avoid, looking for employment in South Africa. That was what I was now doing. And I went about it in the most bizarre manner.

It was as if I had a death wish. I did everything wrong. Of course, when I didn't, it went wrong anyway, all of its own sweet accord.

At the University of Cape Town there was an opening for a junior lecturer in the Department of Social Work. That was one interview I left knowing that I wouldn't get the job. If I had been the interviewer, I would not have given me the job. I don't know what I thought would happen at the interview but, as soon as the woman who was to interview me opened her mouth, my mind closed. Clang. And nothing on the other side could I recall or translate into accessible fact or knowledge that I was supposed to possess. I couldn't even remember the name Freud, never mind Freudian theory and concepts.

Then there were two other close things, both in department stores. With the one I failed to convince a Jewish man that African men would accept my authority. Neither of us brought up the issue of colour: black men have been taking orders from women in South Africa for ages. White women. So his argument was really this: can African men take orders from African women in the job situation? Frankly, I don't know. Neither have been given the opportunity to show their capabilities or lack of them.

And the other department store job? That I did not get this one is still a mystery to me. At the end of what I thought was a good interview I had been told, 'One of two things can happen now. One, we notify you that you've got the job and tell you when to come in for processing, etc. Or, Ha! ha! ha! We send you a letter saying, "We regret ..." Ha! ha! ha!'

The man had laughed, showing an even set of pearly-white teeth. And I had laughed with him. I had laughed for I thought we both understood how preposterous it would be for me to get a letter of regret. I laughed with him. Only, all the while, he was laughing at me. Yes, although I'd been told to expect notification within two weeks, six weeks later (and after at least two telephone calls) the 'We regret' letter came. As I say, that mystified me no end.

I had been back three months. I was back on painfully familiar ground: pennilessness.

Sandile's birthday is on 28 October. This was the first birthday in my immediate family since my return (not counting my fortieth, in August). There could be no celebration.

Early in November, a friend calls: 'Heh, Sindi, we hear you are looking for a job. Nomama says they're looking for someone at her place. She works where the builders get their stamp money, end of the year. This is just pocket money for you, until you find something suitable. Interested?'

'Oh yes, I would be. Where is the place? When should I go?'

'Wait, I'll phone Nomama now and I'll phone you right back. You know children. What do they know? When I said I'd tell you about this job, Nomama wanted to kill me.'

'But why?'

'Eeh, you know Nomama. "Mama, don't you know Aunt Sindi is educated? How do you think she can do a job like this?" And I told her, let me speak to Sindi and hear what she says herself. Now, let me phone her.' And I waited for Ntsiki's call.

The job was with the Industrial Council for the Building Industry, Western Province. During the year, some money is deducted from each worker's weekly pay and the employer adds his contribution. This money is represented in the pay packet by a 'stamp', a coupon. It is these coupons the employee brings to the offices of the Council at year end and redeems them for his 'savings'.

Thus at the end of the year the Council has need for temporary staff to help process the claims. That is the job Ntsiki had called me about: a filing clerk, three hundred rand a month.

I went to see the manager.

'No, Miss Magona. Nomama has told me about you. I don't even have a Master's degree. I'd be embarrassed seeing you do this job and paying you such a pittance.' The elderly gentleman was genuinely upset. I posed a real problem for him. He could see desperation on my face. The job he was offering was suitable for a high-school student. And here I was bringing my Master's degree from overseas.

'Well, Mr J, if you don't give me the job, my three children and I will just starve to death. I mean it. Don't you think that would do more than embarrass you?' I was without shame. Unemployment had made me brazen. Saddled with a conscience, the poor man had no choice. He gave me the job.

I had been working for about four weeks when a former student from my Fezeka Secondary School days, Stephen Ntsane, came to see me. Stephen now worked as a reporter for the *Cape Argus*. He'd heard about my inability to find employment despite my qualifications. Would I give him an interview for an article?

On the appointed day, Steve came, bringing photographers with him. I posed for pictures, answered questions, and more pictures were taken. The article appeared that same day.

The article led, through another friend, to a job as a training officer at a knitwear factory. Mr J was so happy to see me leave the Council that he urged me to take up the position immediately although my time with him was far from over.

'That doesn't matter, Miss Magona,' he said. 'We all knew you wouldn't be with us long and we're delighted your luck has changed.'

To my recollection, this is the only time I have left a job with not only the approval of my boss but his undisguised relief.

December. I began my new job, training machinists to be better, faster, neater at their jobs. I had talked myself into a job I knew nothing about. Desperation. My training is in Organisational Development, making supervisors better at supervision. Here I had to begin by learning the parts of a needle!

One thousand three hundred rand a month – quite a jump in salary: big enough and welcome enough to convince me that I could do the job. After all, I told myself, the principles involved in the two kinds of jobs are the same. Once fear of poverty had convinced me I was capable of doing the job, there was no stopping me from conveying that sense of confident competence to the man who interviewed me. The year closed on a slightly brighter note than I had believed possible even a month before.

1984 began on a delicate pink, the shade of a blooming rose. Soft as a new petal, it was full of promise, hopeful as a woman's dream.

And in March the young year took a dizzying spin. The pink of the new year turned blood red with the birth of a whole new phase.

'Sindiwe? Is that you?' The phone call came a little after lunch.

'Yes?'

'We have something of the utmost urgency here for you. Can you come this afternoon?'

'I'll try.' In pins and needles, I went to my boss and arranged to leave early. As I drove to Cape Town, for once the commanding beauty all round me failed to seize my attention. What could it be? Excitement mated with curiosity in rapturous uncertainty. When I reached my destination an envelope awaited me.

Had it been bigger, the envelope would have resembled the trunk of someone who had just returned from a trip round the world, so covered it was with postage stamps! New York, Washington D.C., Monrovia, Johannesburg, Cape Town.

A contract. A two-year contract. The (by now) forgotten application for a job with the United Nations had yielded a contract. Redemption unexpected. Sweet, sweet salvation.

My knees know by now that the only times I use them are at the peaks and the gorges of my life. I hope they can tell the difference. That night I fell on my knees: 'Dear God!' I prayed, 'if you are so busy looking after me, when will you ever find time to do your work? Tend to your more deserving children? What am I that you have so constantly held me in your loving hand? I, who pay you so little attention.'

Then I remembered the doubts, the lack of trust, the despair. My weakness stabbed me:

'And, Heavenly Father, teach me to know the meaning of your love. Teach me never to doubt your tender caring even in the darkest of nights.'

I wish I could say my faith has been strengthened considerably by the patient, unobtrusive, startling miracles God has worked in my life. I would be less than wholly truthful if I said that.

I wrote to my mother-in-law. Inside her letter I enclosed another, with stamps and money. I asked her to please forward that letter to my husband.

I thought even a father such as my husband had been to his children deserved the chance to say goodbye to them. After all, I was taking them to the other side of the Atlantic.

He phoned. We talked. He came.

Seventeen years before when he left me I had vowed, 'I'll show him.' Now? Now, another me looked at him. I beheld the man who had forsaken me all those many years ago, the man who had refused to answer pointed questions I'd hurled his way. I looked at him, and I found that the need

to gloat had forsaken me. Without my ever taking a con-
scious decision, I had let go even of my anger towards him.
I had long forgiven him. I'd just not known that I had.
Indeed, when I think about it at all, my husband's leaving
me was a lucky break. Of course, I didn't quite see it that
way at the time. He was such a perfect picture of government design. Forty-three years old. And that was his sole
achievement.

The only difference between the man I met and the man
I had last seen in 1966? This man had fine lines, crow's feet,
around his sad, time-dulled eyes. In manner, mood and
maleness he was, as we say in the townships, the same-
same old stew.

Luthando stayed just over a week with us and helped me
bury the past. He had occasionally come across an article
about me in the newspapers, he told me. 'If I hadn't left
you, you would never have done any of the things you have
done,' Luthando said one day, looking at me as any proud
parent would look at his accomplished offspring. I had the
uncanny feeling he was waiting for a big thank-you from
me. But I let in a little shaft of reality: 'Yes, I'm sure I would
not have.... You were far too insecure even to let me go
and take up nursing training, remember?' And arsenic laced
my voice.

Throughout his stay, I looked at my husband and
realised, not for the first time, how lucky I was that he had
left me. Had we stayed together, I doubt I'd still be alive.

But the more scary thing, the thing that makes me break
out in cold sweat, is the mere thought of what I would not
have done with my life. The only ambition I had in 1966,
the year my husband left us, was to go and live with his
parents. Because a town woman was considered of loose
character by village folk, I had then decided to go and console his parents, prove to them they were mistaken in that
judgement, show them my sterling worth.

Therefore, had Luthando not left me, I would have become a migrant's widow, alone eleven months of each year in the village while he earned money to support his family in the mines of Johannesburg as a migrant labourer. That had been my ambition then, to go and be a worthy village wife, pleasing to my in-laws.

Now, in March 1984, life took on a frenetic pace. I ran around like a rabid dog in a thunderstorm. There were the children's passports to organise, visas to apply for, clothes to buy, school records and certificates of vaccination to get. There was furniture to buy: having been in New York before, I'd become fiercely patriotic. Don't ask me why, the Lord knows I was certainly not trying to help the Buy South Africa campaign. However, now that I was on the brink of leaving the country, I discovered that I preferred South African furniture to what I had seen in the States. Call me crazy. Even I cannot understand this passion about a country that has done nothing to foster patriotism in my heart. But then, my umbilical cord is buried somewhere in that country and in no other. Perhaps that is it, the reason for this pull it has on me.

There were other problems not as easy to solve. I was initially leaving the children behind. They would follow as soon as I had found an apartment. Meanwhile, I had to get as much of their affairs organised before I left.

Passports. Of course, although we knew this was a lost cause, we dutifully applied for South African passports. And of course, we were predictably turned down. We were no longer South Africans. Trankeians is what we had become, what we had been forced into becoming, as far as the business of passport goes. So we applied for passports that certified our dispossession, and confirmed our complete lack of power over our own lives.

Ours was thus not an unmixed joy. We were delighted to be leaving. We had our fair share of problems, not least the conflict I was experiencing about the trip itself, the decision to go and work abroad, leaving Mother, siblings, nieces and

nephews. Leaving the country itself. Leaving friends. I wanted to go. I wanted to stay. I couldn't understand why everything had to be so complicated. Why couldn't I have it both
ways? A good job, with reasonable pay, and a life free of
irksome restrictions, safe, supportive of a good living, a
decent life, but without this wrench, without having to up-
root myself?

The severance of the umbilical cord announces the first
breath drawn, and this scene is repeated many a time in the
human drama we call life. Repeated, if in less dramatic
ways. Repeated, for without separation, without this affirma-
tion of being separate, we would stifle each other, wither
and be of no account, like chaff sent hither and thither by
the blowing of the wind.

Almost forty years ago, Mother's illness had led to our
flight from Gungululu to Cape Town. Now I was leaving
Cape Town for New York. Bodily, I was fine. But inside:
that was another matter! If I would ever heal, I needed desperately to go, to leave, to put distance between home and
me. At least, for the time being.

The old people say it is the neighbours who split the
calabash. There is a reason why the ancestors have seen fit
that I dwell among strangers for a while. But I remain ever
of the African soil.

The only fly in my overflowing gourd? Telling my boss, my
benefactor, the good news. The task churned my guts. But it
had to be done.

'Come in! Come in!' he boomed, getting up from his seat
and coming round from behind his large desk. All this I see
from a distance although I can't be more than two feet away
from him, but the tears filming my eyes throw everything far
away from where it really is.

'What can I do for you, my dear?' Did the man have no
eyes? Couldn't he see I was at death's door? I felt faint from

embarrassment and fear. I was filled with shame at being such an ingrate.

'Sir.' This was the first time I'd heard myself calling the man 'Sir'. I hadn't called him that even when he interviewed me for a job I desperately needed. 'Sir,' I repeated, 'I have a job offer from overseas, from New York, the United Nations.' Now I was gushing, breathless. 'And I've come to ask you to release me from....'

'You, wha-aat? But you have a job here!'

'It is not just the job, but everything else that goes with it.' My mind couldn't comprehend his failure to see the obvious. A job in New York spelled a world of difference in the way my children and I would live. Surely even he could see that, surely? I continued, a little firmer now that I felt threatened. He actually might stand in my way. Could he? I didn't know what contractual obligations I was under, what recourse was mine in the event that he insisted on my remaining there. No way! I was not letting such an opportunity slip through my fingers.

'I am sorry, but in March I'll be giving notice of termination.'

'But why? Tell me, why? Aren't you happy here?'

'Well, you see, for starters, the children will be able to go back to school. And, you see, we will live in a real....'

Then I realised I would never make him see.

A good man. He had never imagined himself in my place. He didn't know there was such a place. He didn't know what it was to be me.

* * * * *

So, my child, that is the story of your great-grandmother. That is the story of where you come from.

Here I am, thousands of miles from home, for the ancestors have seen fit that as of now I dwell among strangers. Perhaps, for now, that is the only way I can fulfil my duty to you, my child. The only way I can tell you: This is how it was, in the days of your forebears.

Therefore, forget that I am sitting on a four-legged chair instead of a goatskin or a grass mat. Forget that we meet through your eyes instead of your ears. Listen, for my spirit, if not my flesh, is there with you.

Listen: *'Kwathi ke kaloku,* ... Once it came to pass ..., *kwabe kukho bantu bathile, zweni lithile* ... there lived a certain people in a certain land....'

Other titles by Sindiwe Magona

To My Children's Children
Autobiography / 256 pages
ISBN 1-56656-152-3 $11.95 pb
ISBN 1-56656-163-9 $24.95 hb

Published in 1994 to great acclaim, this powerful autobiography
announced the arrival of a major new black writer. Written as a "letter from
a Xhosa Grandmother," to record her life in South Africa for her
grandchildren so that they do not lose their own history, this is Sindiwe
Magona's account of her eventful first 23 years.

"Magona's memoir is a delightful, poignant, feisty and uplifting story that chronicles, in
a refreshing and authentic voice, what it means to attain womanhood in a society
where patriarchy and apartheid often conspired to degrade and enslave women
economically, domestically, politically, traditionally and sexually."
— *Washington Post Book World*

Living, Loving and Lying Awake at Night
Short Stories / 208 pages
ISBN 1-56656-141-8 $11.95 pb
ISBN 1-56656-147-7 $24.95 hb

Sindiwe Magona's superb collection of short stories brings a full range of
South African women's experience brilliantly to light. From the village
mother leaving her children to work; the maid in service to the white
medem; the black child raped and murdered, *Living, Loving and Lying
Awake at Night* is at once tragic, triumphant, humorous, and sharp, but
above all forcefully empowering.

"Magona is a storyteller centered in her power, convinced of the universal relevance of
what she sees. The effect is felt like the strong South African sun, each story's
momentum like the pounding of a drum."
— *Booklist*

Emerging Voices
New International Fiction Series

The best way to learn about people and places far away

This series is designed to bring to North American readers
the once-unheard voices of writers who have achieved wide
acclaim at home, but were not recognized beyond the borders
of their native lands. It publishes the best of the world's
contemporary literature in translation.

Already published in the series

Pillars of Salt by Fadia Faqir (Jordan) $12.95 pb

The Secret Holy War of Santiago de Chile by Marco Antonio de la
Parra (Chile) $12.95 pb

Sabriya by Ulfat Idilbi (Syria) $12.95 pb

A Balcony Over the Fakihani by Liyana Badr (Palestine) $9.95 pb

The Silencer by Simon Louvish (Israel) $10.95 pb

Under the Silk Cotton Tree by Jean Buffong (Grenada) $9.95 pb

The Stone of Laughter by Hoda Barakat (Lebanon) $12.95 pb

Cages on Opposite Shores by Janset Berkok Shami (Turkey)
$11.95 pb

Living, Loving and Lying Awake at Night by Sindiwe Magona
(South Africa) $11.95 pb

Samarkand by Amin Maalouf (Lebanon) $14.95 pb

The End Play by Indira Mahindra (India) $11.95 pb

The Hostage by Zayd Mutee'Dammaj (Yemen) $10.95 pb

The Children Who Sleep by the River by Debbie Taylor
(Zimbabwe) $9.95 pb

The Dawning by Milka Bajic-Poderegin (Serbia) $14.95 pb

Prairies of Fever by Ibrahim Nasrallah (Jordan) $9.95 pb

War in the Land of Egypt by Yusuf Al-Qa'id (Egypt) $12.95 pb

For a complete catalog please write to:
Interlink Publishing
46 Crosby Street, Northampton, MA 01060
Tel: (413) 582-7054 Fax: (413) 582-7057 e-mail: interpg@aol.com